# REPEAT AFTER ME

# Repeat After Me

REVISED AND UPDATED

## Claudia Black

CENTRAL RECOVERY PRESS

LAS VEGAS

**Central Recovery Press** (CRP) is committed to publishing exceptional materials addressing addiction treatment, recovery, and behavioral healthcare topics.

For more information, visit www.centralrecoverypress.com.

Publisher: Central Recovery Press
3321 N. Buffalo Drive
Las Vegas, NV 89129

23 22 21 20 19 18    1 2 3 4 5

ISBN: 978-1-942094-77-7 (paper)
978-1-942094-78-4 (e-book)

Photo of Claudia Black by Winifred Whitfield. Used with permission.

Every attempt has been made to contact copyright holders. If copyright holders have not been properly acknowledged please contact us. Central Recovery Press will be happy to rectify the omission in future printings of this book.

**Publisher's Note**: This book contains general information about trauma, relationships, and addiction. It represents reference material only and is not intended as medical advice. This book is not a replacement for treatment or an alternative to medical advice from your doctor or other professional healthcare provider. If you are experiencing a medical issue, professional medical help is recommended. Mention of particular products, companies, or authorities in this book does not indicate endorsement by the publisher or author.

CRP's books represent the experiences and opinions of their authors only. Every effort has been made to ensure that events, institutions, and statistics presented in our books as facts are accurate and up-to-date. To protect their privacy, the names of people, places, and institutions in this book have been changed.

*Cover design and interior by Deb Tremper, Six Penny Graphics*

*To the women in my family.*

*To my grandmother, whose strength, energy, and humor I admire.*

*To my mother, who gave me love and the stability that allowed me to grow.*

*And to my sister, Jana, whose childhood and adulthood I've had the honor to share.*

# Table of Contents

**PREFACE** . . . . . . . . . . . . . . . . . . . . . . . . . . . . . . . . . . . . . . . . . . . . . . . . . . . . . . xiii

**A NOTE FROM THE AUTHOR** . . . . . . . . . . . . . . . . . . . . . . . . . . . . . . . . . xvii

**ACKNOWLEDGMENTS** . . . . . . . . . . . . . . . . . . . . . . . . . . . . . . . . . . . . . . . . xxi

**INTRODUCTION** . . . . . . . . . . . . . . . . . . . . . . . . . . . . . . . . . . . . . . . . . . . . . . . .1

**CHAPTER ONE: THE PAST REMEMBERED** . . . . . . . . . . . . . . . . . . . . . . .7

    Family Tree . . . . . . . . . . . . . . . . . . . . . . . . . . . . . . . . . . . . . . . . . . . . . . . . . . .7

    My House . . . . . . . . . . . . . . . . . . . . . . . . . . . . . . . . . . . . . . . . . . . . . . . . . . . .10

    Safe Places . . . . . . . . . . . . . . . . . . . . . . . . . . . . . . . . . . . . . . . . . . . . . . . . . .12

    Talking . . . . . . . . . . . . . . . . . . . . . . . . . . . . . . . . . . . . . . . . . . . . . . . . . . . . . .13

    Not Talking . . . . . . . . . . . . . . . . . . . . . . . . . . . . . . . . . . . . . . . . . . . . . . . . . .14

    Denial . . . . . . . . . . . . . . . . . . . . . . . . . . . . . . . . . . . . . . . . . . . . . . . . . . . . . . .16

    Picture of the Unspoken . . . . . . . . . . . . . . . . . . . . . . . . . . . . . . . . . . . . . .21

    Grounding: Deep Breathing . . . . . . . . . . . . . . . . . . . . . . . . . . . . . . . . . . .22

**CHAPTER TWO: FEELINGS: OLD ENEMIES & NEW FRIENDS** . . . . . . . . .23

    Losing Control . . . . . . . . . . . . . . . . . . . . . . . . . . . . . . . . . . . . . . . . . . . . . . .24

    A Picture of Control . . . . . . . . . . . . . . . . . . . . . . . . . . . . . . . . . . . . . . . . . .27

    Awareness of Feelings . . . . . . . . . . . . . . . . . . . . . . . . . . . . . . . . . . . . . . . .28

    Feelings . . . . . . . . . . . . . . . . . . . . . . . . . . . . . . . . . . . . . . . . . . . . . . . . . . . . .30

    Sadness . . . . . . . . . . . . . . . . . . . . . . . . . . . . . . . . . . . . . . . . . . . . . . . . . . . . .32

    Past Sadness . . . . . . . . . . . . . . . . . . . . . . . . . . . . . . . . . . . . . . . . . . . . . . . . .33

    Expressing Sadness with Tears . . . . . . . . . . . . . . . . . . . . . . . . . . . . . . . . .35

    Picture of Sadness . . . . . . . . . . . . . . . . . . . . . . . . . . . . . . . . . . . . . . . . . . .36

    Sadness Today . . . . . . . . . . . . . . . . . . . . . . . . . . . . . . . . . . . . . . . . . . . . . . .37

    Past Anger . . . . . . . . . . . . . . . . . . . . . . . . . . . . . . . . . . . . . . . . . . . . . . . . . .38

Potential Anger . . . . . . . . . . . . . . . . . . . . . . . . . . . . . . . . . . . . . . . . . . . . . . . . . . . . . .39

Expressing Anger . . . . . . . . . . . . . . . . . . . . . . . . . . . . . . . . . . . . . . . . . . . . . . . . . . . .41

Picture of Anger . . . . . . . . . . . . . . . . . . . . . . . . . . . . . . . . . . . . . . . . . . . . . . . . . . . . . .42

Anger Today . . . . . . . . . . . . . . . . . . . . . . . . . . . . . . . . . . . . . . . . . . . . . . . . . . . . . . . . . .43

Fear. . . . . . . . . . . . . . . . . . . . . . . . . . . . . . . . . . . . . . . . . . . . . . . . . . . . . . . . . . . . . . . . . . .43

Expressing Fear . . . . . . . . . . . . . . . . . . . . . . . . . . . . . . . . . . . . . . . . . . . . . . . . . . . . . . . .46

Picture of Fear . . . . . . . . . . . . . . . . . . . . . . . . . . . . . . . . . . . . . . . . . . . . . . . . . . . . . . . . .46

Fear Today. . . . . . . . . . . . . . . . . . . . . . . . . . . . . . . . . . . . . . . . . . . . . . . . . . . . . . . . . . . . .47

Guilt . . . . . . . . . . . . . . . . . . . . . . . . . . . . . . . . . . . . . . . . . . . . . . . . . . . . . . . . . . . . . . . . . .47

Childhood Guilt. . . . . . . . . . . . . . . . . . . . . . . . . . . . . . . . . . . . . . . . . . . . . . . . . . . . . . . .48

False Guilt . . . . . . . . . . . . . . . . . . . . . . . . . . . . . . . . . . . . . . . . . . . . . . . . . . . . . . . . . . . . .50

Saying No to False Guilt . . . . . . . . . . . . . . . . . . . . . . . . . . . . . . . . . . . . . . . . . . . . . . . .50

Adult Guilt. . . . . . . . . . . . . . . . . . . . . . . . . . . . . . . . . . . . . . . . . . . . . . . . . . . . . . . . . . . . .52

Distinguishing True and False Guilt . . . . . . . . . . . . . . . . . . . . . . . . . . . . . . . . . . . . . .53

Picture of Guilt. . . . . . . . . . . . . . . . . . . . . . . . . . . . . . . . . . . . . . . . . . . . . . . . . . . . . . . . .54

Guilt Today . . . . . . . . . . . . . . . . . . . . . . . . . . . . . . . . . . . . . . . . . . . . . . . . . . . . . . . . . . . .55

Positive Feelings. . . . . . . . . . . . . . . . . . . . . . . . . . . . . . . . . . . . . . . . . . . . . . . . . . . . . . . .55

Expressing Positive Feelings. . . . . . . . . . . . . . . . . . . . . . . . . . . . . . . . . . . . . . . . . . . . .57

Picture of Happiness. . . . . . . . . . . . . . . . . . . . . . . . . . . . . . . . . . . . . . . . . . . . . . . . . . . .58

Happiness Today . . . . . . . . . . . . . . . . . . . . . . . . . . . . . . . . . . . . . . . . . . . . . . . . . . . . . . .59

Defenses as a Mask . . . . . . . . . . . . . . . . . . . . . . . . . . . . . . . . . . . . . . . . . . . . . . . . . . . . .59

Saying Goodbye to a Defense. . . . . . . . . . . . . . . . . . . . . . . . . . . . . . . . . . . . . . . . . . . . .60

Identifying Feelings . . . . . . . . . . . . . . . . . . . . . . . . . . . . . . . . . . . . . . . . . . . . . . . . . . . . .62

Grounding: Circle of Light . . . . . . . . . . . . . . . . . . . . . . . . . . . . . . . . . . . . . . . . . . . . . . .65

## CHAPTER THREE: SELF-ESTEEM: FROM EXTERNAL RAGS TO INTERNAL RICHES

. . . . . . . . . . . . . . . . . . . . . . . . . . . . . . . . . . . . . . . . . . . . . . . . . . . . . . . . . . . . . . . . . . . . . . .67

Self-Esteem of Family . . . . . . . . . . . . . . . . . . . . . . . . . . . . . . . . . . . . . . . . . . . . . . . . . . .67

Self-Image . . . . . . . . . . . . . . . . . . . . . . . . . . . . . . . . . . . . . . . . . . . . . . . . . . . . . . . . . . . . .68

Liking Yourself. . . . . . . . . . . . . . . . . . . . . . . . . . . . . . . . . . . . . . . . . . . . . . . . . . . . . . . . . .69

Self-Value . . . . . . . . . . . . . . . . . . . . . . . . . . . . . . . . . . . . . . . . . . . . . . . . . . . . . . . . . . . . . .70

Name of Worth . . . . . . . . . . . . . . . . . . . . . . . . . . . . . . . . . . . . . . . . . . . . . . . . . . . . . . . . .70

Accepting Compliments . . . . . . . . . . . . . . . . . . . . . . . . . . . . . . . . . . . . . . . . . . . . . . . . .71

Just Say Thanks. . . . . . . . . . . . . . . . . . . . . . . . . . . . . . . . . . . . . . . . . . . . . . . . . . . . . . . . .72

Criticism . . . . . . . . . . . . . . . . . . . . . . . . . . . . . . . . . . . . . . . . . . . 72

Criticizing Others . . . . . . . . . . . . . . . . . . . . . . . . . . . . . . . . . . . . . 74

Shaming Messages . . . . . . . . . . . . . . . . . . . . . . . . . . . . . . . . . . . . 75

Recovery from Shame Attacks . . . . . . . . . . . . . . . . . . . . . . . . . . . . 76

Stilted Success . . . . . . . . . . . . . . . . . . . . . . . . . . . . . . . . . . . . . . . 78

Great Expectations . . . . . . . . . . . . . . . . . . . . . . . . . . . . . . . . . . . . 79

Enjoying Successes . . . . . . . . . . . . . . . . . . . . . . . . . . . . . . . . . . . . 82

Cognitive Distoritions with Counter-Thought . . . . . . . . . . . . . . . . . 82

All-or-Nothing Perspective . . . . . . . . . . . . . . . . . . . . . . . . . . . . . . 84

Present-Day Self-Esteem . . . . . . . . . . . . . . . . . . . . . . . . . . . . . . . . 88

Roles . . . . . . . . . . . . . . . . . . . . . . . . . . . . . . . . . . . . . . . . . . . . . . . 89

The Responsible Child . . . . . . . . . . . . . . . . . . . . . . . . . . . . . . . . . 89

The Placating Child . . . . . . . . . . . . . . . . . . . . . . . . . . . . . . . . . . . 90

The Adjusting Child . . . . . . . . . . . . . . . . . . . . . . . . . . . . . . . . . . . 92

The Mascot Child . . . . . . . . . . . . . . . . . . . . . . . . . . . . . . . . . . . . . 93

The Acting-Out Child . . . . . . . . . . . . . . . . . . . . . . . . . . . . . . . . . . 94

Adult Roles . . . . . . . . . . . . . . . . . . . . . . . . . . . . . . . . . . . . . . . . . . 95

Feminine/Masculine . . . . . . . . . . . . . . . . . . . . . . . . . . . . . . . . . . . 96

Being Feminine . . . . . . . . . . . . . . . . . . . . . . . . . . . . . . . . . . . . . . 96

Being Masculine . . . . . . . . . . . . . . . . . . . . . . . . . . . . . . . . . . . . . . 98

Affirmations . . . . . . . . . . . . . . . . . . . . . . . . . . . . . . . . . . . . . . . . 101

Grounding: Healing Colors . . . . . . . . . . . . . . . . . . . . . . . . . . . . . 102

**CHAPTER FOUR: CREATING A STRONGER SENSE OF SELF** . . . . . . . . . . . . . . . . . . . 103

Needing People . . . . . . . . . . . . . . . . . . . . . . . . . . . . . . . . . . . . . . 103

Pets . . . . . . . . . . . . . . . . . . . . . . . . . . . . . . . . . . . . . . . . . . . . . . . 107

"Needs" Letter . . . . . . . . . . . . . . . . . . . . . . . . . . . . . . . . . . . . . . . 108

I Have Needs . . . . . . . . . . . . . . . . . . . . . . . . . . . . . . . . . . . . . . . . 109

Boundaries . . . . . . . . . . . . . . . . . . . . . . . . . . . . . . . . . . . . . . . . . 111

"No" and "Yes" . . . . . . . . . . . . . . . . . . . . . . . . . . . . . . . . . . . . . . 112

"No" . . . . . . . . . . . . . . . . . . . . . . . . . . . . . . . . . . . . . . . . . . . . . . 113

"Yes" . . . . . . . . . . . . . . . . . . . . . . . . . . . . . . . . . . . . . . . . . . . . . 116

Practicing "No" and "Yes" . . . . . . . . . . . . . . . . . . . . . . . . . . . . . . 119

Inappropriate Behavior . . . . . . . . . . . . . . . . . . . . . . . . . . . . . . . . 122

Intrusive Behavior . . . . . . . . . . . . . . . . . . . . . . . . . . . . . . . . . . . . . . . . . 124

Boundary Violations from Both Sides of the Continuum . . . . . . . . . . . . . 126

Touch . . . . . . . . . . . . . . . . . . . . . . . . . . . . . . . . . . . . . . . . . . . . . . . . . . 130

Meaning of Touch. . . . . . . . . . . . . . . . . . . . . . . . . . . . . . . . . . . . . . . . . . 131

Picture of Touch. . . . . . . . . . . . . . . . . . . . . . . . . . . . . . . . . . . . . . . . . . . 133

Touching People. . . . . . . . . . . . . . . . . . . . . . . . . . . . . . . . . . . . . . . . . . . 133

Apologies. . . . . . . . . . . . . . . . . . . . . . . . . . . . . . . . . . . . . . . . . . . . . . . . 135

Perpetual Apologies . . . . . . . . . . . . . . . . . . . . . . . . . . . . . . . . . . . . . . . . 136

Difficulty Apologizing. . . . . . . . . . . . . . . . . . . . . . . . . . . . . . . . . . . . . . . 139

Apology Letter . . . . . . . . . . . . . . . . . . . . . . . . . . . . . . . . . . . . . . . . . . . . 142

Grounding: Your Five Senses . . . . . . . . . . . . . . . . . . . . . . . . . . . . . . . . . 143

CHAPTER FIVE: FROM MODERATION TO EXCESS . . . . . . . . . . . . . . . 145

Compulsive Behavior . . . . . . . . . . . . . . . . . . . . . . . . . . . . . . . . . . . . . . . 145

Food . . . . . . . . . . . . . . . . . . . . . . . . . . . . . . . . . . . . . . . . . . . . . . . . . . . 146

Eating Habits . . . . . . . . . . . . . . . . . . . . . . . . . . . . . . . . . . . . . . . . . . . . . 146

Money. . . . . . . . . . . . . . . . . . . . . . . . . . . . . . . . . . . . . . . . . . . . . . . . . . 148

Money Today . . . . . . . . . . . . . . . . . . . . . . . . . . . . . . . . . . . . . . . . . . . . . 151

Work. . . . . . . . . . . . . . . . . . . . . . . . . . . . . . . . . . . . . . . . . . . . . . . . . . . 153

Substance Use . . . . . . . . . . . . . . . . . . . . . . . . . . . . . . . . . . . . . . . . . . . . 155

Physical Self-Care. . . . . . . . . . . . . . . . . . . . . . . . . . . . . . . . . . . . . . . . . . 156

Grounding: Palms Up, Palms Down . . . . . . . . . . . . . . . . . . . . . . . . . . . . 157

CHAPTER SIX: RITUALS & SPIRITUAL INFLUENCES . . . . . . . . . . . . . 159

Rituals. . . . . . . . . . . . . . . . . . . . . . . . . . . . . . . . . . . . . . . . . . . . . . . . . . 159

Holidays . . . . . . . . . . . . . . . . . . . . . . . . . . . . . . . . . . . . . . . . . . . . . . . . 159

Christmas (Past). . . . . . . . . . . . . . . . . . . . . . . . . . . . . . . . . . . . . . . . . . . 162

Christmas (Present) . . . . . . . . . . . . . . . . . . . . . . . . . . . . . . . . . . . . . . . . 163

Birthdays. . . . . . . . . . . . . . . . . . . . . . . . . . . . . . . . . . . . . . . . . . . . . . . . 165

Gift Giving and Receiving . . . . . . . . . . . . . . . . . . . . . . . . . . . . . . . . . . . . 168

Bedtime. . . . . . . . . . . . . . . . . . . . . . . . . . . . . . . . . . . . . . . . . . . . . . . . . 169

Dinner. . . . . . . . . . . . . . . . . . . . . . . . . . . . . . . . . . . . . . . . . . . . . . . . . . 171

Dinnertime Picture. . . . . . . . . . . . . . . . . . . . . . . . . . . . . . . . . . . . . . . . . 173

Religion. . . . . . . . . . . . . . . . . . . . . . . . . . . . . . . . . . . . . . . . . . . . . . . . . 175

Early Religious Influence. . . . . . . . . . . . . . . . . . . . . . . . . . . . . . . . . 176

Religion Today. . . . . . . . . . . . . . . . . . . . . . . . . . . . . . . . . . . . . . . . 178

Spiritual Journey. . . . . . . . . . . . . . . . . . . . . . . . . . . . . . . . . . . . . . . 180

Gratitude List. . . . . . . . . . . . . . . . . . . . . . . . . . . . . . . . . . . . . . . . . 181

Grounding: Connecting to a Higher Power. . . . . . . . . . . . . . . . . . . 182

**CHAPTER SEVEN: EMBRACING THE POSSIBILITIES** . . . . . . . . . . . 185

Taking Risks. . . . . . . . . . . . . . . . . . . . . . . . . . . . . . . . . . . . . . . . . . 185

Timeline of Accomplishment. . . . . . . . . . . . . . . . . . . . . . . . . . . . . . 189

The Magic Shop . . . . . . . . . . . . . . . . . . . . . . . . . . . . . . . . . . . . . . . 190

In Closing . . . . . . . . . . . . . . . . . . . . . . . . . . . . . . . . . . . . . . . . . . . 191

# PREFACE

Many years have passed since *Repeat After Me* was first written, and in spite of the years that have passed it still speaks to the heart of those wanting to heal from a troubled childhood. When I began my work over forty years ago I was working with young and adult-age people who grew up in families affected by addiction. I spoke about how one learns to not talk honestly at a very young age. You don't talk honestly because you do not think you will be believed, heard, or supported. You fear repercussions; you feel as if you are being disloyal. Or maybe you don't think there is anyone to talk to. You learn not to show your feelings, and in time you emotionally disconnect from yourself. You learn you cannot rely on others, you cannot trust them to be there for you, and some people learn to even distrust themselves. These are the infamous rules: *Don't Talk, Don't Feel, Don't Trust*. I spoke about the family roles that people take on to bring greater stability to their lives: the responsible hero child, the adjuster (lost) child, the placater, the acting-out (scapegoat) child. These children develop coping mechanisms that for the most part do not draw attention, and they are not seen as children in need. Often the impact of growing up in an addictive family system doesn't blatantly show itself until adulthood. Those responses carried into adulthood often morph into primary issues such as codependency, depression, anxiety, and addiction to a process or substances.

In the 1980s and '90s the issue of trauma was being recognized by myself and others pioneering the work with adult children from families impacted by addiction but without the language of trauma that has evolved since that time. Looking back I realize that *Repeat After Me* was and is addressing the narrative of one's trauma experience. It offers insight into naming the trauma and begins the process of grief work and the beginning of creating a new narrative for your life.

Since the original publication, we now have science that supports the value of journaling and writing exercises. *Repeat After Me* is based on the value of writing as a therapeutic process. Research by James Pennebaker, PhD, shows that writing about life's stresses helps you heal from both physical and emotional ailments. Recalling memories, good and bad, comes easier when you put them down in words. Writing your stories frees up buried emotions and thoughts, giving rise to epiphanies about how you have lived your life. People solve problems while writing and become more satisfied with their circumstances. While I believe you and I have very likely known that, it is nice to see this work validated.

As you proceed to work on healing, let me offer a framework for trauma: *trauma* is a Greek word that means *wound; a hurt or a defeat*. It is not a disease or a condition. It is the body and brain's response to a painful, overwhelming, or terrifying experience that overwhelms the ability to cope with the resulting rush of feelings and thoughts. Trauma freezes the moment in time and implants powerful thoughts, emotions, and physical sensations, which remain embedded in your body and brain—potentially for years or even decades—until the trauma is addressed and healed. It may result from events that almost anyone would find disturbing, such as a car accident, a natural disaster such as a fire or hurricane, or the witnessing of a violent act. Other traumas are not so blatant, and often go unrecognized as to the effect they can have on you. They could be things such as harsh or unfair criticism, rejection, being bullied, being shamed or demeaned, being yelled at, ignored, disrespected or discounted; betrayal, lack of empathy from a parent, unrealistic expectations, acrimonious divorce or inappropriate boundaries (too rigid, too permissive, disconnected or enmeshed). In reality, people actually experience more traumas within their own family system than outside of it. That is whom this workbook is written for.

Those who suffer trauma experience a great sense of loss. This may mean the loss of trust, connection to others, innocence, truth, reality, safety, boundaries, or the ability to feel calm or relaxed or comfortable in your own skin.

Trauma creates a repetitive and profoundly disempowering internal belief. That ultimate core belief is shame, the painful feeling that comes with the belief that who you are is not okay; you are not worthy; you are not of value.

When I first wrote *Repeat After Me* I referred to a four-step process for healing.

1.  Explore the past
2.  Connect the past to the present
3.  Challenge the beliefs
4.  Learn the skills

Today I have expanded these steps to be what I refer to as "layers."

## Layer One: Grounding

Grounding is essential in the healing of familial trauma. Grounding will help you stay present. Grounding skills are learnable, tried-and-true tools to help your nervous system regulate and calm the part of your brain where the flight, fight, or freeze responses dominate. Grounding skills help you to stay calm, focused, and alert so that you can feel emotions fully, process and tolerate and, when appropriate, let them go. In fact you may already practice some of them. Many are fun, pleasurable, or rewarding, and most are free or inexpensive.

Forms of grounding include martial arts, tai chi, yoga, meditation, creating art (drawing, sculpting, coloring, etc.), crafting (knitting, needlepoint, woodworking, etc.), dancing, singing, chanting, writing (journaling, poetry, etc.), gardening, playing or working with animals, or spending time in nature. As you work through the exercises in this workbook, grounding helps you have greater inner stability. While you are strongly encouraged to engage in these practices, each chapter here offers grounding meditations or visualizations.

## Layer Two: Exploring the Narrative

Many of the exercises in *Repeat After Me* will help you explore what happened, how you responded, and what you experienced as support. These exercises in large part are about undoing denial. If you continue to deny the reality of your past you will use the skill of denial in present-day situations. Exploring the past is an act of empowerment. It relieves you of the burden of holding on to defenses you no longer need. It helps you to discover or reclaim your power, to recognize and make healthy choices, and to be able to talk honestly without fearing rejection or punishment.

This layer of healing has often been perceived as blaming others. It is not. Accepting the truth is not the same as assigning blame. When you acknowledge that you were wounded and how you were wounded, you are helping yourself to heal, not exacting revenge on anyone else.

## Layer Three: Moving into Your Emotions

Feelings are something you may have spent years trying to avoid, but that you picked up this workbook says you are getting ready, you are prepared and willing to take a journey that you know will offer healing but that involves feelings. Keep in mind that feelings are an important part of who you are, but they neither rule you nor define you. If you have been cut off from feelings for a long time, they may seem foreign or unsettling when you begin to experience them again. This is normal. Remind yourself that you have kept these emotions at bay for years. Now you are learning a healthier way to experience them.

The goal is not to get rid of feelings, but to learn how to identify them; to use them as signals and cues to indicate your needs; to learn how to tolerate them without engaging in self-defeating thoughts and behaviors; and to put them into realistic perspective. Just the act of writing, a tool that taps into your limbic system where your emotional self resides, allows you to be more open to the experience of feelings.

## Layer Four: Connecting the Past to the Present

This layer involves asking questions such as: How does my history impact me in various areas of my life? My self-esteem? My partner relationships? My parenting? My friendships? My work choices? Etc. This brings you into today's focus.

## Layer Five: Uncovering and Challenging Internalized Beliefs

Without a recovery process it is likely you are operating according to a belief system you developed long ago. These beliefs may have helped you survive when you were young, but now they no longer serve their purpose. In fact they probably get in the way of how you would like to live your life.

## Layer Six: Learning New Skills

You get to keep all of the useful skills you learned growing up, but most likely there are many life skills you didn't learn, and some of the exercises will encourage you to practice new skills as well as create them.

## Layer Seven: Creating a New Narrative

This is the essence of *Repeat After Me*. With the insight you gain from these exercises you will learn to challenge your unhealthy beliefs, learn new skills, and recognize the choices available to you. Creating a new narrative is taking ownership of how you want to live your life.

# A NOTE FROM THE AUTHOR

The mid-1980s, when *Repeat After Me* was first published, was a time when adult children of addicted families were coming out of the closet by the thousands. Until that time these were adults who were silently making their way through adulthood not understanding why they were so unsatisfied and unhappy when "everything seemed okay," or why nothing "was ever enough." For many, there was a chronic gnawing sense that something was missing. For others, it was more blatant. It was depression, rage, addiction, and other compulsive behaviors. A great number of people happily took on the identity of being an ACA or ACOA (Adult Child of Alcoholic). They were grateful to have a framework to understand and conceptualize their experience and a language to voice their experiences. Yet what was true for this particular population could be generalized to people from other types of troubled families. They were from homes where there was abuse, other forms of addiction, compulsive behaviors, or mental illness—homes that for various reasons were characterized by loss and shame.

As adults began asking how their childhood was influencing their present-day life, the focus was on insight and understanding rather than blame. It has been my contention that people repeat the life scripts of their family as a result of internalized beliefs and behaviors that were either modeled for them or were part of surviving their early life experiences. You cannot put a painful past history behind you without first owning it. It is not enough to say that you came from an addicted or an abusive family. You must go beyond that acknowledgment to see how your internalized beliefs and behaviors have shaped you to be who you are today. *Repeat After Me* was written in the spirit of offering all who were raised in troubled families a process of self-exploration, insight, and healing that can lead to positive change in their lives.

This is not a book that explains how problems come to be as much as it is a workbook that takes you through a process of letting go of hurtful beliefs and behaviors. While insight is often the precursor to change, insight alone is not enough for most people to create change. People need to believe they deserve positive change and they need to develop skills that make change occur. This edition of *Repeat After Me* is designed to support your belief in your personal worth and help to identify and develop your skills.

Adults who were raised in troubled families need to walk through a four-step process for healing to occur:

1.  **Explore your past.** For the purpose of owning it and to undo your denial process so you can take off the mask of denial in your present-day life. Exploring the past means owning the losses and grieving the pain associated with past history. The purpose in this lies in putting the past behind you.

2.  **Connect your past history to your present-day life.** You connect the past to the present by asking questions like, *How does the past influence my life today? How does it influence me as a parent? How does it influence me in relationships? How does it influence me in my work?* And so forth. Then the questions become more specific. They may take the form of, *How does the fact it was never safe for me to show anger influence me today as a parent? How does the fact it was never safe for me to make decisions influence my decision-making in the workplace? How does the fact I was constantly criticized impact how I feel about myself as an adult?*

3.  **Identify and challenge the beliefs internalized from your upbringing.** Ascertain which of these beliefs are useful to maintain, and which are hurtful and need to be let go of. In recognizing the beliefs you need to let go of, you need to create more constructive beliefs in their place. For example, you might toss out, *No one wants to listen to what I have to say*, and replace it with, *My thoughts and opinions are important and of value.*

4.  **Learn skills.** So often the skills you need to learn are basic, such as learning to listen, to recognize options, to negotiate, to identify and express feelings, and to set healthy limits. It is in this step you create positive change.

The knowledge that comes from owning your past and connecting it to the present is vital to developing an appreciation for the strength of both your defenses and your skills. It also helps you to lessen your shame and not hold yourself accountable for pain you have carried. When you understand there are reasons for why you have lived your life as you have, and that it is not because there is something inherently wrong with who you are or that you are not "bad," that understanding fuels ongoing healing. The change you want to create in your life is most directly made through letting go of old, hurtful belief systems, and the learning of new skills. It is my hope that *Repeat After Me* guides you in this process.

In previous writings I used the term *adult child* to refer specifically to adults who grew up in homes affected by parental alcoholism. In *Repeat After Me*, however, its meaning is broadened to include any adult raised in a home environment where he or she experienced many losses—as a child and/or teenager—whether as a result of an identifiable problem or of more nondescript family challenges and difficulties. Please be advised that for simplicity and clarity I use the male pronoun when referring to a singular person.

While this workbook was written to provide guidance and structure for people to explore important issues on their own, it is my hope that you have someone in your life with whom you can share what you are learning about yourself. Healing cannot be done in isolation. Today, with often-limited access to psychotherapy resources, *Repeat After Me* is an especially valuable tool. However, if you are in therapy or counseling, doing these exercises outside of therapy and bringing what you are learning about yourself into your sessions can help you get more out of the experience.

(From the 1995 edition)

# ACKNOWLEDGMENTS

During the time I contemplated and wrote *Repeat After Me*, I received a great deal of support that I would like to acknowledge.

Steve Wielachowski, Diane Murry, Diane Coll, and Bill Reid were most helpful in the formulation of the exercises.

I am appreciative of the feedback provided by Patty Shryock, Mike Shryock, Diane Morshauser, Marci Taylor, Dave Landers, Victoria Danzig, Mary Carol Melton, Beth Reynolds, Wynn Bloch, and Allan Campo. A special thanks to Allan for his musical notes that kept my spirits up when they faltered.

Marguerite Tavarez worked diligently on the word processor in the creation of *Repeat After Me*. Thank you for your feedback, editing, patience, and support.

Roz Schryver was a delight to work with and I am grateful to her for her editing assistance on earlier editions of *Repeat After Me*.

Becky Jackson, Tammy Stark, and Debbi Mahon deserve a hearty thank you for their daily efforts in the production and distribution of all my work.

I offer my gratitude to Amy Morris, for her typing, editing, and feedback on the second edition of *Repeat After Me*; and to Tammy Stark, for her never-failing belief in the value of this piece of work.

I have many friends who are a significant part of my personal recovery process, but I would like to pay special tribute to Lorie Dwinell, who was instrumental in helping me to begin the path that led to the freedom and choices I experience today. Also to my friend, Jael Greenleaf, for being an ongoing supporter and personal friend; and to Lou Stoetzer, whose acceptance and direction I value and trust.

Once again, I owe thanks to my late husband, Jack Fahey. I thank you for your feedback, your earlier edition rewrites, and your willingness not to tire with another one of my dreams.

As I look over the original acknowledgments I think fondly of those who were vital to the original creation of *Repeat After Me*. Their feedback and support has influenced, to date, nearly 300,000 readers. For the original 300,000 readers, I admire your courage and willingness, and am glad to have been a part of your lives.

# INTRODUCTION

Once upon a time you were a child, a fact that has important bearing on your life today. As an adult, you may try to ignore your life as a child and discount the impact it may have had on your adult life. *Repeat After Me* was written to be of help to you, the reader, whose parents were not consistently able to attend to your needs, who were unable to help you believe you were special, and were unable to give you a sense of emotional safety as you grew from childhood and adolescence into adulthood. These are parents in homes in which there is no identifiable problem—homes where a family avoids showing feelings, homes where there is little nurturing, homes where rules are rigid rather than fair and flexible, and homes where time is not given to the children. If these dynamics occurred in your family, it is likely you came into adulthood not feeling very good about yourself, having difficulty trusting people, having difficulty identifying your needs and allowing those needs to be met. These things can cause great difficulty in your ability to be close to others and create problems in your personal or professional life.

If addiction, physical and/or sexual abuse, or mental illness were present in your family, the consequences are likely even greater. It is very common for adults who come from such families to have difficulty asking for what they want, difficulty trusting, difficulty identifying or expressing feelings, and to have great fears of being rejected resulting in a tremendous need to seek approval. While an overdeveloped sense of responsibility is often characteristic of these adult children, many are not able to enjoy their accomplishments. They have great fear of "losing control" while demonstrating an extreme need to control. Identifiable problems such as addiction and physical and sexual abuse often repeat themselves in the following generations. Whether or not there was an identifiable problem in the family, these children have experienced significant losses during childhood.

There is considerable pain connected to such losses, and it has negative and unhealthy effects in adulthood—unless it is addressed. While many people are able to reflect on their childhood and describe situations that were blatantly hurtful, other people experienced hurt by what did not occur—what wasn't said as opposed to what was. To have a parent ignore you can be as hurtful as having a parent verbally ridicule you.

*Repeat After Me* is intended to:

1.  Help you recognize how your present life is influenced by your past,

2.  Allow you to release the parts of the past you'd like to put behind you, and

3.  Most importantly, to enable you to take responsibility for how you live your life today.

Freedom from the past means no longer having your life dominated by your childhood years. It means no longer living in fear. In the process of freeing themselves, people begin to say,

- "I'm angry that . . . "
- "I needed . . . "
- "No, . . . "
- "It wasn't right that . . . "
- "I was only a kid when . . . "
- "Thank you . . . "
- "I'm lovable . . . "
- "It does matter . . . "

This can be said without blame and judgment.

*Repeat After Me* was not written to put blame on your parents. I believe all of our parents did the best they knew how to do. Yet, our parents' ability to raise us was oftentimes limited because of some significant trauma in their own lives. This trauma may have been physical, financial, or emotional. For the most part, parents love their children. However, many lacked the ability to consistently show that love. If they didn't love us, it was because they didn't know how to love—it was not about us. They may have wanted it to be different but they did not have the ability to make it different, nor were they able to ask for help or accept help.

It is common for adults to feel guilt about wanting to reflect on how the way they were parented as children affects their adult life, or they want to minimize it, often saying, "compared to many others, it wasn't that bad for me." No matter how severe another person's situation may have been, your own losses and the pain they inflicted are valid and deserving of attention. In determining whether or not you need to address these issues, it is suggested that you do not compare your situation to anyone else's. What has occurred in your life is yours—your sadness, fears, broken promises, silent punishments, absent parents.

## LOYALTY

Adults often feel guilty when talking about their past because they believe they are being disloyal to their family. When you do the exercises in this workbook, you are not saying that your parents are bad people;

you aren't saying that you don't love them. You are describing things that took place—attitudes, behaviors, and feelings. What you write about is your perception of what has occurred. You are addressing the past rather than keeping it inside. When you begin to release the past, the energy it takes to keep the past and its pain within yourself can be used for healing in the present. There is a significant psychological relief in writing and in talking. When you talk openly, you are more apt to receive validation from others and less likely to experience the "alone-in-the-crowd" syndrome. Talking honestly is the first step in creating a bond with others. If there is an act of disloyalty, it is most apt to be disloyalty toward yourself—for not owning your experiences.

## MEMORY RECALL

In some exercises you will be asked to respond to any memories you have at a very young age, such as birth to five years. That option is there for those who have such memory. Keep in mind that it is normal to have little recall of events until approximately five years of age. As you get older, recall becomes increasingly clearer. There will be some of you who may not remember much of your childhood at all.

There does not need to be a single traumatic event to cause lack of recall; it could be the chronicity of threats that can be so overwhelming that allows the memory portion of the brain to shut down.

Do the exercises in this workbook to the best of your ability. Exercises such as these do much to facilitate your memory. You will remember more of your childhood as you go through *Repeat After Me*. Try not to become preoccupied with retrieving whatever information doesn't seem to be available to you. It is not necessary for you to have total recall to move forth in recovery.

## SHARING WITH FAMILY MEMBERS

After completing a few of the exercises, you may be tempted to speak to other family members about your past. This is not necessarily recommended.

Unless your parents have experienced a recovery process dealing with their own problems and/or they feel good about themselves and no longer continue old behaviors, they will not understand what you are saying. They will repeat their old patterns of defense: ignore you, scream, blame, cry, or give you token acknowledgment. Do not expect them to say, "I'm sorry." "I love you." "I was wrong."

When parents are in recovery themselves, their lives are very different than they were, and they may be able to hear what you say. But even still, it will hurt, and they probably won't like it. So, if your goal is to tell them without hurting them, that is not realistic. Rather than remaining quiet, a better and more realistic approach is to share your experience with your parents and allow them to feel their own pain.

This kind of sharing demands great honesty on your part, guided by the following questions:

- What do you want to tell them?
- Why do you want them to hear that?
- How will it help you to say that to them?
- Are you saying this to hurt them?

You may tell yourself you just need to say certain things out loud. If so, out loud to whom? Anyone? Or out loud to your parents?

If you choose to share your thoughts and feelings with them it is best to keep your expectations low. What do you want to happen or expect to happen when you share with them? Are your expectations realistic? Remember that you can share only what you want—it's not an all-or-nothing proposition.

However, most adult children will never experience their parents participating in a recovery process of their own. In many cases, the parents of adult children have died; in others, they may have no interest in contact. Fortunately, many issues can be resolved without parental involvement. Even when it is not possible to resolve issues directly with your parents, it is possible to change your behavior, say what needs to be said, and come to a place of self-acceptance.

In early recovery, be cautious about sharing your new awareness and self-discoveries with your brothers and sisters. Adult children tend to give to others before themselves, and to share newfound awareness before they have fully integrated their new understanding. If you have been in a recovery process (e.g., therapy, self-help groups) for a period of time and the life changes you have made are healthy, solid, and stable, this is now a more impactful time to share what you've discovered with siblings. As with parents, the key to sharing with siblings is to identify what is important to tell them and why, and have realistic expectations of the results of your sharing.

Keep in mind that different family members experience life within the same family very differently. Children have different personalities from birth, and many variables affect the development of their personalities. Moreover, each child enters the family at a different place in the family's history, including the progression of various challenges and illnesses that plague families. For instance, over time, parents went from not being addicted and codependent into early-stage addiction, and then progressed to middle-stage, and on to late-stage. Those children who have access to either parent prior to the onset of addiction and codependency or during earlier stages may have had access to healthier parenting—and in turn, more consistency and predictability. This leads to a greater sense of security and more ability to trust. In these families, typically the middle and younger children have less opportunity to experience a healthy (even if it is sometimes short-lived) family environment. As a result, each child has different perceptions and learned a different style of survival.

All that being said, for now try not to be overly concerned about what and when you share. Move through the workbook and become comfortable with your new awareness. In time you'll know what, if anything, you need to share with your family members.

## DO IT WITH SUPPORT

It is suggested you have a support system that is aware of what you are working on. It is important that you verbalize to others what you discover and how you feel as you make progress. Consider who in your life is supportive of your desire to grow. This may be a friend you write to or talk to frequently. This could be someone at work. This may be a family member. Look to get the support you need where it is given genuinely. Many readers will find their greatest support in professional counseling and/or mutual-aid/self-help groups such as Adult Children of Alcoholics, Al-Anon, Nar-Anon, Codependents Anonymous, Overeaters Anonymous, etc. One of the greatest supports would be a *Repeat After Me* group where all participants walk through the workbook together.

## ON YOUR WAY

*Repeat After Me* was designed to help you take the steps in a process toward a greater sense of self-awareness, self-love, and a more comfortable way of life.

As you complete these exercises, many of you will experience newfound feelings and thoughts. This may be difficult, but it will become more comfortable in time. Some of the exercises will produce great emotion, others will not. Some will quickly produce great insight; with others you may see the value only after a period of time. Please do them all. It is strongly suggested that you complete them in their specific written order. Do them slowly. Take them seriously. At times you'll complete questions fully, other times this will not be the case. There are no right or wrong answers.

It is strongly recommended that you respond to all of the exercises in writing, rather than just thinking about them or responding in your head. The physical act of writing makes you more committed to the process of healing and will promote your healing more effectively. Have additional paper available in the event you need additional space for your written responses to the exercise questions. As you move though this workbook, remember that what you write is *yours*—your experiences, your thoughts, your feelings. It is your perception, your reality that is important. And, keep in mind that you don't have to make any big decisions regarding your past or present as a result of your emerging awareness or feelings. Just do the exercises. Receive the information. Try not to be judgmental of yourself. Know that you are not alone—this workbook was written because of the needs of many people.

This workbook is not meant to be completed in its entirety in one sitting. The more you are able to be honest about your feelings, the more you will be able to assess the speed that is best for you. This process can be very intense and have deep impact, so it is suggested that you work on the exercises no longer than one hour per sitting. It is also suggested you devote a minimum of one hour every week to this workbook. To move through the exercises too quickly may prevent you from feeling the impact of your growing awareness and understanding, while moving too slowly may inhibit the momentum that is so valuable for your healing.

# CHAPTER ONE
# THE PAST REMEMBERED

## FAMILY TREE

### EXERCISE 1

To better understand your family system, it is helpful to have a mental picture of your family. To the best of your ability, fill in the names of your family members. For many people, this exercise reminds them of how little they know of their familial history. If you can't complete some of the names, simply be aware there are missing pieces to your history. What does that mean or imply to you? You may choose to seek out others to assist you in filling in the blanks.

**FAMILY TREE**

| MOTHER'S SIDE | FATHER'S SIDE |
|:---:|:---:|
| **Maternal Grandparents** | **Paternal Grandparents** |
| Grandmother/Grandfather | Grandmother/Grandfather |
| _____  _____ | _____  _____ |
| Name Aunts with Spouses | Name Aunts with Spouses |
| _____  _____ | _____  _____ |
| Name children | Name children |
| _____ | _____ |
| _____ | _____ |

_____     _____

_____     _____

_____     _____

_____     _____

_____     _____

_____     _____

_____     _____

_____     _____     _____     _____

_____     _____

_____     _____

_____     _____

_____     _____

Name Uncles with Spouses          Name Uncles with Spouses

_____     _____     _____     _____

Name children          Name children

_____     _____

_____     _____

_____     _____

_____     _____

_____    _____    _____    _____

_____    _____                               _____

                           _____                               _____

                           _____                               _____

                           _____                               _____

_____    _____    _____    _____

                           _____                               _____

                           _____                               _____

                           _____                               _____

                           _____                               _____

| 2nd Husband<br>(Stepfather) | MOM | DAD | 2nd Wife<br>(Stepmother) |
|---|---|---|---|

_____    _____    _____    _____

_____                                                          _____

| Sisters & Brothers<br>(Include Yourself) | Spouse | Children | |
|---|---|---|---|

_____    _____    _____    _____

                                                       _____    _____

_____    _____    _____    _____

                                                       _____    _____

_____    _____    _____    _____

                                                       _____    _____

_____      _____      _____      _____

                                    _____      _____

_____      _____      _____      _____

                                    _____      _____

_____      _____      _____      _____

                                    _____      _____

Indicate with a circle (O) the names of family members you know have experienced alcohol or other drug problems.

Check (✓) the names of family members you know have experienced eating disorders.

Mark with an X (✕) the names of family members you know were physical abusers and/or were abused.

Indicate with a square symbol (▢) the names of family members you know were incest perpetrators and/or incest victims.

Indicate with a star (★) the names of family members you know experienced other identifiable dysfunctions, and name the problem.

Indicate by circling the person's name(s) those family members you have held a strong positive regard for. When you are done do some writing as to why you feel the positive attachment.

## MY HOUSE

### EXERCISE 2

Sit in a relaxed position. Take a deep breath—in and out—and then do it again, more slowly this time. Now, in your memory, go back in time, back to the years when you were growing up. Picture the home you most remember from those years. What community is it in? How old were you when you lived there? Who lived in this home with you? With a large piece of paper, draw the floor plan of the home that came into your memory.

Label all of the rooms.

Consider the following questions, and note your responses on the floor plan you have drawn.

Which rooms did you like? _____

_____

Which rooms didn't you like? _____

_____

Where did you go when you wanted to be alone? _____

_____

Where did you go when you were angry?_____

_____

Where did you go when you were sad?_____

_____

With whom did you tend to spend the most time in your home? _____

_____

With whom did you tend to spend the least time in your home? _____

_____

Was being in your home different on weekends compared to weekdays? _____

If yes, how was it different? _____

_____

_____

Has that pattern repeated itself in adulthood? If yes, how? _____

_____

On another large piece of paper, draw the floor plan of the home you live in today and answer the same questions.

## SAFE PLACES

### EXERCISE 3

Sometimes people who grow up in challenging families go to a particular place at home for a sense of safety—a closet, under the bed, in a tree house, under the porch, etc. Did you have any such place? Write about this place. Describe where it was and the security you felt when you were there.

_____

_____

_____

_____

_____

_____

_____

# TALKING

## EXERCISE 4

While healthy boundaries give people the ability to pick with whom and where they share their feelings and thoughts, for many children it was safer (psychologically and sometimes even physically) to be quiet about what occurred at home. One of the consequences of that is people then develop a silent tolerance for the inconsistencies and untruths, and then internalize the feelings associated.

Reflect on people you may have talked to about problems at home when you were a young child and teenager. Check the frequency with which you can remember talking about problems to your:

| | Never | Once | Occasionally | Often |
|---|---|---|---|---|
| Mother | ☐ | ☐ | ☐ | ☐ |
| Father | ☐ | ☐ | ☐ | ☐ |
| Stepmother (name) _____ | ☐ | ☐ | ☐ | ☐ |
| Stepfather (name) _____ | ☐ | ☐ | ☐ | ☐ |

| | Never | Once | Occasionally | Often |
|---|---|---|---|---|
| Brother (name) _____ | ☐ | ☐ | ☐ | ☐ |
| Brother (name) _____ | ☐ | ☐ | ☐ | ☐ |
| Sister (name) _____ | ☐ | ☐ | ☐ | ☐ |
| Sister (name) _____ | ☐ | ☐ | ☐ | ☐ |
| Grandparent(s) (name) _____ | ☐ | ☐ | ☐ | ☐ |
| Other Family Member (name)_____ | ☐ | ☐ | ☐ | ☐ |
| Teacher (name) _____ | ☐ | ☐ | ☐ | ☐ |
| Counselor (name) _____ | ☐ | ☐ | ☐ | ☐ |
| Clergy (name) _____ | ☐ | ☐ | ☐ | ☐ |
| Friend (name) _____ | ☐ | ☐ | ☐ | ☐ |

Neighbor (name) _____     ☐     ☐     ☐     ☐

Other (name) _____     ☐     ☐     ☐     ☐

List the people in your life today with whom you are willing to share your problems.

1. _____

2. _____

3. _____

4. _____


## NOT TALKING

### EXERCISE 5

Certain issues may have been present in your family life as a child and a teenager that prevented you from talking about problematic areas of your life. Circle those that were true for you:

- I felt ashamed.
- I felt disloyal, as if I was betraying my family.
- I was embarrassed.
- I didn't understand what was occurring well enough to talk about it.
- I was afraid I wouldn't be believed.
- I was specifically instructed not to talk.
- It was insinuated in nonverbal ways that I should not talk.
- It seemed as though no one else was talking.
- I believed something bad would happen if I talked.
- I came to believe that nothing good would have come from talking.

If, as an adult, you still have difficulty talking about your childhood and adolescence, put a (✓) by the statement(s) that apply to you today.

If you do talk about your childhood, note to whom it is you talk:

_____

_____

_____

_____

_____

_____

- If, as an adult, you still feel a sense of shame when talking about your growing-up years, try to understand that you weren't at fault and your parents would have liked it to have been different. Talk about your childhood with people you trust.
- Should you still feel a sense of guilt when talking with others, trust that you are not betraying your parents, your family, or yourself; you are giving voice to the unhealthy and unhelpful experiences in your home growing up.
- Should you still feel a sense of confusion about your childhood, that's probably an accurate description of how life has been for you—confusing. When attempting to explain irrational behavior in a rational manner, it will often sound confusing. Talking will help you develop greater clarity.
- Should you still have difficulty understanding what occurred in your family, read further and continue talking about it.
- Should you still fear that you won't be believed, a great deal of information is available that will substantiate your experiences as not being entirely unique.
- If you were instructed (specifically or nonverbally) *not* to talk about what happened at home, that instruction was motivated by fear or guilt. You don't have to live that way any longer.
- That you are reading this workbook indicates that you are aware that others are talking about their history and how they have been affected. Talking is a necessary part of letting go of the pain of the past.
- If you have experienced something negative from people you spoke with in the past, today you are free to choose a healthier support system.
- If you have been conditioned to believe that "nothing good comes from talking," put faith in the belief that it is only when you finally begin to speak your truth that you will be able to put the past behind you and experience the joy of the present.

Now ask yourself, "What are the areas of my life I hesitate to tell others about and what are the beliefs that get in the way?"

_____

_____

_____

_____

_____

_____

_____

## DENIAL

One of the clearest definitions of denial came from a nine-year-old child who said, "Denial is when you pretend things are different than how they really are."

Family denial occurs when family members minimize, discount, or rationalize what happened within the family system. They deny out of a combination of fear and hopelessness. Family members learn to minimize, discount, or rationalize in their attempts to bring stability to their lives. In order to deny, people are required to be dishonest. Honesty will sabotage the active addict's use of alcohol and other drugs, and will sabotage family members' attempts to pretend that everything is okay when it is not. When applied in traumatic situations, honesty will often cause discomfort and possibly uproar. But the truth is that in the long run honesty will make it possible for people to see that help is needed.

Children learn to minimize, discount, and rationalize for fear of the consequences should they speak the truth. Oftentimes when a child speaks the truth, he is told that what he sees is not accurate: "Your mom's not drunk, your mom's depressed." "Dad's sick from the flu" (sick from drinking). "Your dad didn't really hit you that hard. He's just under a lot of stress" (black eye, broken rib).

This parental action of rationalizing and discounting serves as the model for the child who will begin his or her own process of rationalizing, discounting, and denial. When you have lived with chronic denial, your ability to own your truth is seriously damaged.

## EXERCISE 6

In recognizing each family member's denial, it is possible to see how the whole family environment has been affected. Think about times your family discounted or minimized situations or feelings:

I can remember the time (Mom)    minimized
discounted _____
rationalized

_____

I can remember the time (Mom)    minimized
discounted _____
rationalized

_____

I can remember the time (Dad)    minimized
discounted _____
rationalized

_____

I can remember the time (Dad)    minimized
discounted _____
rationalized

_____

_____

I can remember the time (Stepparent)   minimized
                                        discounted _____
                                        rationalized

_____

_____

I can remember the time (Stepparent)   minimized
                                        discounted _____
                                        rationalized

_____

_____

I can remember the time (Brother)       minimized
                                        discounted _____
                                        rationalized

_____

_____

I can remember the time (Brother)       minimized
                                        discounted _____
                                        rationalized

_____

_____

I can remember the time (Sister)        minimized
                                        discounted _____
                                        rationalized

_____

_____

I can remember the time (Sister)        minimized
                                        discounted _____
                                        rationalized

_____

_____

Looking back in time, was denial a way of life for your family?

_____

_____

_____

## EXERCISE 7

Reflect on your childhood and adolescence and complete the following sentence about separate occasions:

I can remember the time I pretended (minimized or discounted) about . . .

1. _____

_____

when in reality . . . _____

_____

2. _____

_____

when in reality . . . _____

_____

3. _____

_____

when in reality . . . _____

_____

4. _____

_____

when in reality . . . _____

_____

Checking to see if you carry what is often a finely tuned skill into adulthood, complete the following:

Today I minimize (rationalize or discount) . . .

1. _____

_____

when in reality . . . _____

_____

2. _____

_____

when in reality . . . _____

_____

3. _____

_____

when in reality . . . _____

_____

4. _____

_____

when in reality . . . _____

_____

As you work through these exercises, you'll begin to recognize your denial. This awareness will allow you to be more honest, to better identify your feelings, to better identify your needs, and will provide you with opportunities for greater self-care.

By eliminating denial you will see things more clearly for what they are, which will help alleviate problems that denial allows to continue and worsen. Honesty allows you to begin to live more freely in the here and now.

## PICTURE OF THE UNSPOKEN

### EXERCISE 8

While many feelings and situations were discounted in your family, others were not talked about or addressed at all. Do a collage about the things you and other family members saw, heard, or felt that no one ever mentioned or did anything about. Collages are made by cutting out pictures, words, and/ or letters from magazines or other print publications and creating images that make a statement and express your feelings.

To make a collage, you need: 1) a 14" × 17" piece of paper, 2) Scotch-type tape, 3) a pair of scissors, and 4) three to five magazines. Nearly any magazine can be used, but an assortment of different magazines is suggested. Allot 60–90 minutes to do your collage. (Complete it in one sitting.) It is usually easier to begin your collage by flipping through a magazine and being open to what you see rather than looking for specific pictures or words. Part of the value in doing a collage is finding words or pictures that jump out at you, that describe your experiences and feelings.

Remember, this is *your* collage. Only you will interpret the pictures or words. There is no right or wrong way to do this. When making your collage, try not to be influenced by anyone else's perceptions of what happened in your family. Ask yourself what *you* felt was important.

EXAMPLES:
1) A picture of an automobile may represent being with a parent when he/she was drinking and driving and never talking about it.

2) A picture of an attractive person may represent your own attractiveness that was never acknowledged by your parent.

3) A picture of a Christmas tree may remind you of a particular family fight during the holidays that was never discussed again.

4) A picture of a trophy may represent your being selected for a school or sports honor, yet your parents didn't acknowledge or attend the awards ceremony.

When situations and feelings are not acknowledged, not only are they discounted, but you yourself will feel devalued. This is very destructive to your self-image. Your willingness to identify what has not been previously acknowledged is an important step toward valuing yourself.

## GROUNDING: DEEP BREATHING

Stand up and place your feet shoulder-width apart, so you are stable. Take a few deep breaths.

Relax your shoulders and drop your hands to your sides. Let your arms and hands dangle.

Take in a long, deep breath through your nose. Then blow it out through your mouth like a big gust of wind.

Repeat for several minutes.

This activity can be especially helpful when you feel overwhelmed by whirling thoughts or strong feelings.

# CHAPTER TWO

# FEELINGS: OLD ENEMIES & NEW FRIENDS

Many people have difficulty identifying their feelings. The beliefs that get in the way of identifying and expressing feelings are influenced by gender-based stereotypes and culture, in addition to one's family. Having difficulty identifying feelings usually comes from a history where showing feelings was unsupported and often punished. Or certain feelings were reinforced more than other feelings. While you may be aware of one or two of your feelings, you may not be able to identify other feelings. For example, you may be so consumed with anger that you are unable to feel sadness, disappointment, or fear. Or, you may feel so guilty that you are unable to identify anger.

You might have been told that you weren't "supposed to feel that way," or you were "wrong" to feel the way you did. Many times, your feelings were ignored. Probably the greatest reason people stop expressing their feelings is the belief that nothing good comes from it. As an adult, being unable to express feelings contributes to feeling depressed, having difficulty in relationships, and being unable to get your needs met. It results in negative defenses such as rage, the need to control self and/or others, or self-medication via alcohol or other drugs, food, sex, shopping, gambling, etc.

As you use this workbook, you will experience many feelings that have been dormant for a long time. It is possible that you will be aware of feelings of loneliness, anger, sadness, fear, and a general sense of vulnerability. When you have a history of repressing your feelings and now those feelings begin to rise to the surface, you may interpret those sensations as "feeling crazy" or that "something is wrong." You are allowing yourself to be vulnerable, and being vulnerable can be scary. The goal is fourfold: to have feelings; to know what they are when you have them; to be able to express them in a healthy manner; and, just as importantly, to be able to tolerate (be with) them.

The following exercises will help you to identify specific feelings and understand what these feelings represent.

## LOSING CONTROL

Before you can better understand your feelings, it is important to talk about "control" and, more specifically, about "losing control." When people begin to experience feelings, they often fear losing control. This section will address what "loss of control" means for you.

## EXERCISE 9

*Control* can be manifested both externally and internally. Externally, people control by exerting authority or force, or through the manipulation of people, places, and things. This control is often an attempt to bring greater order and stability to your life. When you do not have the structure you need, you attempt to create it for yourself. An example of this is when you set the bedtime for younger brothers and sisters and literally tuck them in. Perhaps as a child, by default you became the household top sergeant, dividing the household responsibilities among the kids and making sure the house had some semblance of cleanliness. Such children are the ones who make sure the bills are paid, the neighbors are told the right stories, and that schoolwork gets signed as needed.

While many children try to control their environment in a way that provides greater psychological safety, some are only internal controllers. Internal control is when you minimize your needs and withhold your feelings. While you may not have control over anything outside of yourself, at least you have some control over whether or not you set yourself up for disappointment and greater reprimand. By not asking for anything, by diminishing your needs, by not expressing your feelings, you may feel a greater sense of safety and security. Many people are both external and internal controllers.

To better understand what *control* has meant for you, complete the following sentences:

Giving up control in my family would have meant _____

_____

Giving up control in my family would have meant _____

_____

Giving up control in my family would have meant _____

_____

Giving up control in my family would have meant _____

_____

If you have difficulty with this exercise, another way to benefit from it is to describe the controlling behavior (remember, your controlling behavior was a way to protect yourself, so don't be judgmental).

For example:

Not taking care of my mother would have meant _____

_____

Not doing the grocery shopping would have meant _____

_____

Not holding in my feelings would have meant_____

_____

If you were raised in an abusive or highly authoritarian environment, it may be hard to believe you had any kind of control. Be open to the possibility that you may have developed a strong sense of inner control. Whether or not you were controlling as a child or a teen, you may compensate for not ever having had any control when you were younger by being highly controlling today as an adult.

Past experiences often interfere with your ability to let go of control today. And you must be willing to let go of some control to experience a healing process. In ascertaining your internal perception or fear of what it would mean to let go of control, you have the opportunity to deal with a foundational issue in your healing process. The issue of control is vital to much of your healing.

Take time to do the previous writing exercise and to talk with someone you trust about what giving up control would have meant in your earlier years.

Then, do the following exercise. Know that you may find yourself writing some of the same things you wrote in the previous exercise. That is because, as adults, people often repeat their past experiences.

**EXERCISE 10**

Create a comfortable setting, relax, and close your eyes. Visualize what you fear might happen should you give up control.

Today, giving up control means_____

_____

_____

_____

_____

_____

_____

_____

_____

_____

For most people, losing control means showing their feelings. Adults who have repressed feelings often fear that when they cry, they will become hysterical, or when they are angry, they will explode and perhaps hurt someone or themselves in their rage. Control is often perceived as an all-or-nothing issue. Examples of people's perceptions of losing control include:

- "I fear that I may physically hurt someone."
- "I fear I will lose friendships and offend others."
- "I will start to cry and not be able to stop."
- "If I let out my rage I'll start breaking furniture or hurting people."
- "I fear I'll say something hurtful to someone."

Look at the statements you wrote earlier regarding losing control.* Where do those thoughts and feelings come from? How old are they? How likely is it that those fears would be realized? So often your fears are greater than the reality. If these fears are real, what do you need to do to find a safe way to let go of some control?

*If you have been hospitalized for depression or have physically hurt someone else in anger and have fears that it will happen again, it will be important and helpful for you to share such thoughts about "losing control" with a trained, helping professional.*

## A PICTURE OF CONTROL

### EXERCISE 11

Draw a picture or do a collage on what giving up control means to you. You choose whether the focus is giving up control today or during your growing up years, or possibly both.

EXAMPLES:

1) A picture of a cake advertisement might demonstrate the powerlessness one feels around food.

2) A picture of a small dirty child might represent that you took control of housekeeping and parenting your siblings so outsiders wouldn't recognize what was going on at home.

3) A picture of money may represent your use of money to exert control today.

As you need to, refer back to Exercise 8 for instructions on creating a collage.

It is not suggested that you give up all control, but rather *some*. As you let go of some control, you actually become more empowered. You will find flexibility where there has only been rigidity. As many readers who have begun their healing process have already discovered, when they begin to let go of some control, they begin to experience more opportunities to relax, to play, to let go of the burden of carrying the world on their shoulders. You have the opportunity to know yourself better, to be honest with yourself and others, to trust, to listen, and to connect. It is when you let go of control this process begins to take on spiritual meaning. You cannot experience a spiritual healing process until you are willing to let go of control.

Because fears of giving up control are activated when people begin to get in touch with their feelings early in this healing process, you may find it helpful to give yourself messages that help you feel greater safety as you give up control. For example, you may want to counter your old messages with messages such as:

• Losing control *does not mean* becoming hostile; being angry can be okay.

• Losing control *does not mean* becoming hysterical; one can find relief in tears.

- Losing control *does not mean* "bombing someone with nasty words," but letting them know what my needs are, which will be more helpful to me.

Other helpful messages include:
- "I don't need to be in control at all times."
- "I don't need to be in control if it means denying my wants, my feelings, or my sense of spontaneity."

List two messages that will be helpful to you in giving up some control.

1. _____

_____

2. _____

_____

## AWARENESS OF FEELINGS

Painful feelings are more likely to lessen when you are able to talk about them. When you don't express them, they accumulate. Present-day disappointments, losses, anger, and fear can become intertwined with old disappointments, losses, anger, and fear, making it difficult to separate old issues from new issues.

As you become aware of and express your feelings, keep in mind that having a feeling does not mean you need to act on it. How you feel and what you do with those feelings are separate issues. For now, just be aware of the feeling. Try to view your feelings as a part of you. Let the feelings be your friend. Feelings hurt the most when they are denied, minimized, or discounted. As you own your feelings and begin to feel them, know they aren't there to rule you, but to be cues and signals that tell you something.

### EXERCISE 12

What are the messages (those others have told you and those you have told yourself) that interfere with your willingness to show feelings?

1. _____

_____

2. _____

_____

3. _____

_____

4. _____

_____

Where did you get these messages?

_____

_____

_____

What is the price you pay for maintaining these messages?

_____

_____

_____

_____

_____

## EXERCISE 13

Being new at owning your feelings, it is important for you to know the value of being able to identify and express them.

Some of these benefits are:

- When I know what my feelings are and am more honest with myself, I then have the option of being more honest with others.

- When I am in touch with my feelings, I am in a better position to be close with other people.
- When I know how I feel, I can begin to ask for what I need.
- When I am able to experience feelings, I feel more alive.

List four more reasons it is of value *to you* to be able to identify and express feelings:

1. _____

_____

2. _____

_____

3. _____

_____

4. _____

_____

## FEELINGS

### EXERCISE 14

You have many feelings, some you are willing to expose, and others you choose to keep hidden. Identify the most significant feelings you had in each of the age ranges below. Indicate the feelings you expressed, as well as the ones you kept to yourself. The list of feelings is only a partial one, so feel free to add your own.

Be aware that people often have more than one feeling at a time and those feelings may seem contrary to each other. You can love and hate, be sad and angry, be fearful and happy at the same time. This does not mean you are crazy; it means you have reasons to be both fearful and happy, angry and sad, or to hate and love.

**FEELINGS**

| | | | | |
|---|---|---|---|---|
| love | anger | bravery | confusion | anxious |
| hurt | gloom | shyness | happiness | embarrassment |
| fear | guilt | patience | moodiness | disappointment |
| hate | caring | jealousy | excitement | encouragement |
| worry | warmth | joy | frustration | discouragement |
| shame | sadness | resentment | lonely | |

| Ages | Expressed | Unexpressed |
|---|---|---|
| Before 6 | _____ | _____ |
| | _____ | _____ |
| | _____ | _____ |
| 6–11 | _____ | _____ |
| | _____ | _____ |
| | _____ | _____ |
| 12–17 | _____ | _____ |
| | _____ | _____ |
| | _____ | _____ |
| 18–24 | _____ | _____ |
| | _____ | _____ |
| 25–34 | _____ | _____ |
| | _____ | _____ |
| | _____ | _____ |

35–44    _____        _____

_____        _____

_____        _____

45–54    _____        _____

_____        _____

_____        _____

55–64    _____        _____

_____        _____

_____        _____

65 +     _____        _____

_____        _____

_____        _____

## SADNESS

There is always a great deal of loss in a home where you do not get the hugs you need, the praise you deserve, or the reliable consistent parenting provided in healthy families.

With loss there is sadness, and with sadness there are often tears. Feeling sad and crying is a natural part of being human. If you did not receive validation for your sadness—if you experienced negative responses when expressing sadness—you probably learned to control the expression of such feelings.

Many adults find themselves without the ability to cry. Others find that after years of seldom crying, they cry frequently and are unable to identify the reasons why there seems to be an over-abundance of tears. The next few exercises are designed to enable you to identify your sadness and to help you to better understand how you perceive crying.

## PAST SADNESS

### EXERCISE 15

Sadness in families is often caused by certain things that occurred or were said. Yet for many, sadness is caused by what *wasn't* said or what *didn't* occur, such as for all the times a parent didn't show up for school events, or from never being told that you were loved.

Complete the following sentence:

When I was a child or teenager, I can remember feeling sad (whether or not anyone else knew that you were sad) about:

1. _____

_____

2. _____

_____

3. _____

_____

4. _____

_____

Check the behaviors that describe what you did as a child when you felt sad:

☐ Cried when I was alone

☐ Cried in front of others

☐ Went to bed

☐ Took a walk

☐ Told someone about my sadness

☐ Other (fill in) _____

☐ Other (fill in) _____

When I felt sad, my mom usually: (Check the most appropriate answers)

_____ Never noticed

_____ Noticed, but ignored it

_____ Made me feel embarrassed or ashamed

_____ Made me feel better

_____ Other (fill in) _____

When I felt sad, my dad usually: (Check the most appropriate answers)

_____ Never noticed

_____ Noticed, but ignored it

_____ Made me feel embarrassed or ashamed

_____ Made me feel better

_____ Other (fill in) _____

If there was a particular person—a brother, sister, or other significant person in your life that responded to your sadness (either negatively or positively), describe how they responded:

_____

_____

_____

_____

_____

_____

_____

_____

_____

## EXPRESSING SADNESS WITH TEARS

### EXERCISE 16

This exercise is designed for adults who have difficulty expressing sadness with tears and for people who fear their tears.

Complete the following sentences:

When I cry, I_____

_____

When I cry, I_____

_____

When I cry, I feel _____

_____

When I cry, I feel _____

_____

If people see me cry, I would _____

_____

If people see me cry, they would _____

_____

If you were unable to complete the first lines of the previous exercise because you never cry, complete the following statements:

I never cry because_____

_____

I never cry because_____

_____

If I ever did cry, _____

_____

If I ever did cry, _____

_____

I might have felt better if I'd cried when _____

_____

I might have felt better if I'd cried when _____

_____

## PICTURE OF SADNESS

### EXERCISE 17

Draw a picture or do a collage of your sadness. Your sadness can be from your past and present experiences.

EXAMPLES:
1) A picture of a smiling person may represent what you did to mask your sadness as a child.
2) A picture of the color or the word "blue" may describe your sadness.

3) A picture of a cloud may represent an intense amount of sadness and tears within you.

4) A picture of a woman may represent your mother, who reminds you of your greatest source of sadness.

Again, as needed, refer back to Exercise 8 for instructions on creating a collage.

## SADNESS TODAY

### EXERCISE 18

After noting present-day sadness, on the right-hand side of the page list people that you have shared the specific sadness with or a person you are willing to share that sadness with now.

Today I feel sad about:                                                     Name

1. _____     _____

_____

2. _____     _____

_____

3. _____     _____

_____

4. _____     _____

_____

## PAST ANGER

People often have difficulty admitting and expressing anger because they believe getting angry means the cessation or withdrawal of love. Feeling angry doesn't have to mean a lessening of love. Being angry doesn't mean hating or even disliking whatever it is you may be angry about. Feeling angry means you feel angry—it does not need to have additional meaning.

However, if you have no difficulty identifying your anger and are frequently angry, you may want to focus on your fear or sadness. Intense anger often indicates that other feelings are hidden—covered up by the anger. Fear and sadness are among the feelings most frequently masked.

There are things that have happened for which you may always feel anger about, and the goal is not to eliminate the anger but to put it in its proper perspective so that it doesn't interfere with your life.

## EXERCISE 19

Along with sadness, a great deal of anger is present when there has been significant loss in your life. There are reasons for your anger—the many things that were said or happened, as well as the words never said that you needed to hear, the times your parents weren't there for you, and the lack of validation you experienced. Yet in learning to survive, much of that anger may have been denied, minimized, and discounted. Complete the following sentence:

When I was a child or teenager, I can remember being angry about (whether or not anyone else knew that you were angry):

1. _____

_____

2. _____

_____

3. _____

_____

If you have difficulty identifying your anger, you may want to think in terms of the words "frustrated," "disgusted," "irritated," or "upset." Sometimes changing the word lessens the power of meaning, making it easier to accept. If that helps, go back to the previous exercise and try it again, only with your new words.

## POTENTIAL ANGER

### EXERCISE 20

If you still have difficulty identifying your anger, try thinking of five things that took place in your childhood and adolescence that you *could have* been angry about. You may not have gotten angry or frustrated at the time, but the situation was frustrating and the potential for anger was there. Another way of looking at it is to imagine a young child at age 5, 7, 9, etc., and put him or her in your family in the same situation. Make a list of what this child could be angry about:

_____

_____

_____

_____

_____

Check the behaviors that describe what you did as a child with your anger:

☐ Pouted

☐ Screamed (at whom?)

☐ Was sarcastic

☐ Told the person with whom I was angry directly about my anger

☐ Hit harder on the ball field (or other sport)

☐ Ate to stuff my anger

☐ Ran away

☐ Other (fill in) _____

☐ Other (fill in) _____

When I was angry, my mom usually: (Check the most appropriate answers)

_____ Never noticed

_____ Noticed, but ignored it

_____ Made me feel embarrassed or ashamed

_____ Made me feel better

_____ Other (fill in) _____

When I felt angry, my dad usually: (Check the most appropriate answers)

_____ Never noticed

_____ Noticed, but ignored it

_____ Made me feel embarrassed or ashamed

_____ Made me feel better

_____ Other (fill in) _____

If there was a particular person—a brother, sister, or other significant person in your life that responded to your anger (either negatively or positively), describe how they responded:

_____

_____

_____

_____

_____

_____

_____

## EXPRESSING ANGER

### EXERCISE 21

As described earlier, people often have difficulty dealing with their anger. Many times they have no awareness of it. They may be frightened of their own anger, they may be frightened of other people's anger, or they may have so much anger they feel explosive.

It is important to explore how you perceive your anger. Complete the following sentences:

When I am angry, I _____

_____

When I am angry, I _____

_____

When I am angry, I feel _____

_____

When I am angry, I feel _____

_____

If people see me angry, I'd feel _____

_____

If people see me angry, I'd feel _____

_____

When people get angry, I_____

_____

If you were unable to complete the first five lines of the previous exercise because you are never angry, complete the following statements:

I'm never angry because _____

_____

I'm never angry because _____

_____

If I ever got angry, I'd _____

_____

If I ever got angry, I'd _____

_____

I might have felt better if I'd gotten angry when_____

_____

I might have felt better if I'd gotten angry when_____

_____

## PICTURE OF ANGER

### EXERCISE 22

Draw a picture or do a collage of your anger. This anger is to be from your past and present experiences.

EXAMPLES:
1) A picture of a volcano may represent how explosive and frightening your anger is to you.
2) A picture of a bottle of alcohol may represent that you often drink to deal with your anger.

3) A picture of a dog depicts being mad at your dad for giving your dog away when you were a child.

4) A picture of a car may typify another form of escape for you when you are angry.

Refer back to Exercise 8 for instructions for creating a collage.

## ANGER TODAY

### EXERCISE 23

After noting present-day anger, on the right-hand side of the page, list people that you have shared the specific anger with or a person you are willing to share that anger with now.

Today I feel angry about:                                                   Name

1. _____        _____

_____

2. _____        _____

_____

3. _____        _____

_____

4. _____        _____

_____

## FEAR

Many people grow up with chronic fear. When growing up with chronic stressors, fear is often denied. These fears, recognized or not, are usually carried into adulthood. In time, the denial lessens and many people become aware of a great deal of fear but are unable to identify what it's about or where it comes from. This fear is often referred to as "unidentifiable" or "free-floating" fear. This fear may appear episodically (appearing quickly and powerfully, then leaving almost as mysteriously), or be pervasive (ever-present).

## EXERCISE 24

Make a list of six situations that took place for you during your growing up years that you remember as being fearful whether or not you expressed that fear:

1. _____

_____

2. _____

_____

3. _____

_____

4. _____

_____

5. _____

_____

6. _____

_____

Check the behaviors that describe what you did as a child when you felt afraid:

☐ Acted like I was not afraid

☐ Cried

☐ Got angry

&#9633; Hid (Where?)_____

&#9633; Told someone about my fear (name) _____

&#9633; Other (fill in) _____

&#9633; Other (fill in) _____

When I was afraid, my mom usually: (Check the most appropriate answers)

_____ Never noticed

_____ Noticed, but ignored it

_____ Made me feel embarrassed or ashamed

_____ Made me feel better

_____ Other (fill in) _____

When I was afraid, my dad usually: (Check the most appropriate answers)

_____ Never noticed

_____ Noticed, but ignored it

_____ Made me feel embarrassed or ashamed

_____ Made me feel better

_____ Other (fill in) _____

If there was a particular person—a brother, sister, or other significant person in your life that responded to your fear (either negatively or positively)—describe how they responded:

_____

_____

_____

_____

## EXPRESSING FEAR

### EXERCISE 25

To better understand how you experience fear as an adult, complete the following sentences:

When I am afraid, I _____

_____

When I am afraid, I _____

_____

When I am afraid, I _____

_____

If people knew I was afraid, _____

_____

If people knew I was afraid, _____

_____

## PICTURE OF FEAR

### EXERCISE 26

Draw a picture or do a collage of your fear from your past and present experiences.

EXAMPLES

1) A picture of a person of the opposite sex may indicate that you are afraid of the opposite sex.

2) A picture of the word *no* may represent how difficult you find it to say no.

3) A picture of a hand may represent getting hit.

4) A picture of a cartoon showing a person walking on a tightrope may represent how fearful life is for you.

Refer back to Exercise 8 for instructions for creating a collage.

## FEAR TODAY

### EXERCISE 27

After noting your present-day fears, on the right-hand side of the page list people that you have shared the specific fear with or a person you are willing to share that fear with now.

Today I feel afraid about:                                                                                 Name

1. _____          _____

_____

2. _____          _____

_____

3. _____          _____

_____

4. _____          _____

_____

## GUILT

Guilt is a feeling of regret or remorse about something you have done or not done. While guilt is a healthy emotion that facilitates social conscience, for many people it is distorted, particularly if they were raised in a dysfunctional family. Often when problems occur, family members blame each other: spouses and partners blame each other, parents blame children, children blame parents, children blame each other. Young children, because they are defenseless, most readily accept and internalize the blame.

Many people may not be aware that they internalized guilt as intensely as they have until they see themselves acting out the guilt by chronically apologizing and taking care of others at the expense of their own needs, or succumb to depression.

## CHILDHOOD GUILT

### EXERCISE 28

Check the boxes of the family members with whom you feel guilty for things that took place when you were a child:

☐ Mom                                             ☐ Brother (name) _____

☐ Dad                                             ☐ Brother (name) _____

☐ Sister (name) _____            ☐ Brother (name) _____

☐ Sister (name) _____            ☐ Other (name) _____

☐ Sister (name) _____            ☐ Other (name) _____

For each box checked, give two reasons for your feelings of guilt. Example: "I felt responsible for Mom and Dad's arguing because they often argued about me." "I felt responsible for my brother getting hit. I was older and should have been able to stop my dad." or "I felt responsible for not being able to make my mom happier; I could have gotten better grades in school."

_____

_____

_____

_____

_____

Check the behavior that describes what you did when you felt guilty as a child:

☐ Ate to stuff my feelings of guilt

☐ Hid (Where?)_____

☐ Apologized

☐ Cleaned the house

☐ Tried to act "really good"

☐ Other (fill in) _____

☐ Other (fill in) _____

Check the most appropriate responses that describe what happened when you felt guilty:

When I felt guilty, my mom usually:

_____ Never knew

_____ Reinforced my guilt by blaming me for things I did not do

_____ Made me feel even more guilty

_____ Punished me even if I was not at fault

_____ Made me feel that I was not responsible, therefore, helping to lessen my guilt

_____ Other (fill in) _____

When I felt guilty, my dad usually:

_____ Never knew

_____ Reinforced my guilt by blaming me for things I did not do

_____ Made me feel even more guilty

_____ Punished me even if I was not at fault

_____ Made me feel that I was not responsible, therefore, helping to lessen my guilt

_____ Other (fill in) _____

## FALSE GUILT

Because children have limited mental, physical, and emotional resources, a major part of parenting involves physically and psychologically protecting the children so they feel "safe." Children need security, love, happiness, and honesty in order to grow and feel good about themselves. Yet in many homes parents are not able to meet these needs on a consistent basis. In dysfunctional families where parents are unable to take care of the basic needs of the children, those children often attempt to fill the void by assuming certain parental responsibilities.

But remember, these are young children who do not yet have the ability to act as responsible adults. Not only do parents often ask children (directly and indirectly) to take responsibility for things which adults should be responsible for, they often insinuate that their children are the *cause* of their (the adults') problems. Children usually believe their parents "know everything" and accept what their parents tell them.

As a result, young children have a distorted view of their power—they come to believe they have more power to affect people, places, and situations than they do. This results in feelings of false guilt for things far beyond their control and an overwhelming sense of powerlessness.

## SAYING NO TO FALSE GUILT

### EXERCISE 29

It is important to gain a realistic perspective of situations that you have the power to affect. You may have a distorted perception of where your power lies and as a result live with a lot of false guilt. True guilt is remorse or regret for something you have done or not done. False guilt is taking on guilt for things that are unrelated to what you have or haven't done, and sometimes assuming the feeling of guilt for someone else's behavior and actions.

Because this is usually a lifelong habit, it is important to go back and delineate historically what you were and were not responsible for. That will help you become more skilled in recognizing and stopping your patterns of taking on false guilt.

Reflect back on your childhood and adolescence and consider the things you feel guilty about, and say "no" to each situation. Then say, "No! I wasn't responsible for _____," or "No! It wasn't my fault, my obligation."

Write "No!" in each blank and then continue by finishing the sentence:

1. _____, I was not responsible for_____

_____

when he/she _____

2. _____, I was not responsible for_____

_____

when he/she _____

3. \_\_\_\_\_, it wasn't my fault when _____

_____

4. \_\_\_\_\_, it wasn't my fault when _____

_____

5. \_\_\_\_\_, it wasn't my duty or obligation to_____

_____

6. \_\_\_\_\_, it wasn't my duty or obligation to_____

_____

7. \_\_\_\_\_, I was only partially responsible for _____

_____

8. \_\_\_\_\_, I was only partially responsible for _____

_____

Now write about anything else you might feel guilty about that wasn't your fault:

_____

_____

_____

_____

_____

# ADULT GUILT

## EXERCISE 30

List names of significant people in your adult life. Then circle the names of those about whom you are feeling guilty:

1. _____     5. _____

2. _____     6. _____

3. _____     7. _____

4. _____     8. _____

For each person circled, give two reasons that prompted your guilt. For example: "I felt responsible when my husband wrecked the car because I should have gone with him and been the driver." "I feel guilty for leaving my wife." "I feel guilty for taking sick days from work when I was not really sick."

_____

_____

_____

_____

_____

_____

_____

_____

To help distinguish true and false guilt note **TG** for True Guilt or **FG** for False Guilt next to your examples.

## DISTINGUISHING TRUE AND FALSE GUILT

### EXERCISE 31

Recognizing that we only have the power to affect our own behavior, not the behavior of others, fill in the following sentences:

Today, I'm not responsible for _____

when he/she _____

Today, I'm not responsible for _____

when he/she _____

It isn't my fault when _____

_____

It isn't my fault when _____

_____

It isn't my duty or obligation to _____

_____

It isn't my duty or obligation to _____

_____

I am only partially responsible for _____

_____

I am only partially responsible for _____

_____

I am responsible for _____

_____

I am responsible for _____

_____


## PICTURE OF GUILT

### EXERCISE 32

Draw a picture or do a collage of your guilt from your past and present experiences. It can be false or true guilt.

EXAMPLES:

1) A picture of an obese person eating a gallon of ice cream represents what you do with guilt.
2) A picture of a child in leg braces depicts your guilt for the car accident in which your children were injured.
3) A picture of a bottle of liquor represents tremendous guilt related to addiction.
4) A picture of a coffin represents the guilt you feel for acts of self-harm.

Refer back to Exercise 8 for instructions for creating a collage.

## GUILT TODAY

### EXERCISE 33

After noting present-day guilt, on the right-hand side of the page list people that you have shared the specific guilt with or a person you are willing to share that guilt with now.

Today I feel guilty about:                                         Name

1. _____    _____

_____

2. _____    _____

_____

3. _____    _____

_____

4. _____    _____

_____

## POSITIVE FEELINGS

### EXERCISE 34

As important as it is to be able to identify feelings that are painful, it is just as important to be in touch with feelings of pleasure.

Check the behaviors that describe what you did as a child when you felt happy:

☐ Laughed out loud

☐ Sang

☐ Walked in the woods

☐ Spent time with someone

☐ Spent time with my dog

☐ Wrote poetry

☐ Other (fill in) _____

☐ Other (fill in) _____

When I felt this way, my mom usually:

_____Never noticed

_____Noticed, but ignored it

_____Did something to lessen the feeling

_____Shared, supported, or participated in the feeling

_____Other (fill in) _____

When I felt this way, my dad usually:

_____Never noticed

_____Noticed, but ignored it

_____Did something to lessen the feeling

_____Shared, supported, or participated in the feeling

_____Other (fill in) _____

If there is a particular person—a brother, sister, or other significant person in your life that responded to this feeling (either negatively or positively), describe how they responded:

_____

_____

_____

_____

_____

_____

Make a list of words that connote positive/warm feelings. Now complete the following sentence:

When I was child or teenager, I can remember feeling—*excited, happy about, anticipatory, giddy, love toward, loved* (whatever words you used)—when:

1. _____

2. _____

3. _____

4. _____

## EXPRESSING POSITIVE FEELINGS

### EXERCISE 35

This exercise is designed to assist you if you have difficulty expressing love, acceptance, joy, etc.

Today, I don't let others know when I experience positive feelings because:

_____

_____

_____

_____

What beliefs are you operating on that get in the way of expressing your positive feelings? What is the price you are paying as a result?

_____

_____

_____

_____

_____

_____

_____

_____

_____

_____

_____

_____

## PICTURE OF HAPPINESS

### EXERCISE 36

Draw a picture or create a collage of happiness from your past and present experiences.

EXAMPLES:

1) A picture of the forest reminds you of the feelings of peace and solitude you felt when walking through the forest as a teenager.

2) A picture of a group of people all singing together represents a feeling of belonging that you experience with certain friends (this feeling doesn't have to have anything to do with singing).

3) A picture of a family in a car reminds you of positive family time.

4) A picture of books represents your enjoyment of learning.

Refer to Exercise 8 to refresh yourself on instructions for creating a collage.

## HAPPINESS TODAY

### EXERCISE 37

Note what makes you happy today and list people that you share these moments with.

Today I experience (*your positive-feelings words*) when:         Name

1. _____    _____

_____

2. _____    _____

_____

3. _____    _____

_____

4. _____    _____

_____

## DEFENSES AS A MASK

### EXERCISE 38

When feelings are too painful or uncomfortable, it is normal to create various defenses to keep them at a distance. This may ultimately interfere with your ability to identify and feel certain feelings. Unfortunately, when the defenses are chronically used and become a way of life, they interfere with healthy functioning. By knowing your defenses, you are in a better position to identify your uncomfortable feelings.

What feelings are the easiest for you to show in front of people?

_____

_____

_____

What are the more difficult feelings for you to show people?

_____

_____

_____


Taking one of those difficult feelings, when you begin to experience it, what do you do to defend against it? Do you mask it with another feeling, e.g. cover fear or sadness with anger? Do you isolate or intellectualize? Do you eat or use humor? Or, do you do other things?

_____

_____

_____

_____

_____


By recognizing what you do to mask your feelings, you are in a better position to identify your more hidden feelings. For instance, when you catch yourself intellectualizing, and you know you use that as a defense to mask your fear, you can now ask yourself if you are actually afraid. If you acknowledge that you use sarcasm to mask your anger, you can own the anger when you hear your own caustic remarks.


## SAYING GOODBYE TO A DEFENSE

### EXERCISE 39
The following list identifies common defenses that many develop as a form of emotional protection.

Common defenses are:

- Anger
- Silence
- Intellectualizing
- Smoking
- Busyness
- Magical thinking

- Rage
- Humor
- Isolation
- Food
- Smiling
- Sarcasm

- Ambivalence
- Minimizing
- Perfectionism
- Work
- Other _____
- Other _____

Pick a defense you frequently use that gets in the way of how you want to live your life and is interfering with your ability to be honest with yourself or others. This is a defense that has outlived its usefulness.

Now, write a letter of goodbye to that defense. Begin by writing:

*Dear Defense (Silence, Smoking, etc.),*

Thank the defense for how it has served you. In essence, honor it. Then tell the defense how it is hurting you, causing you pain in your life. Lastly, tell it that you need to let it go.

An example:

> *Dear Perfectionism,*
> *I want to thank you for the help you have given me over the years. I needed you when I was a child. I was so scared and didn't want anyone to know. I had to do the right thing or teachers wouldn't have noticed me. I didn't want anyone to think there was anything wrong at home. Because of you, Perfectionism, I got a lot of positive attention and I learned to get a lot done.*
> *But now you are getting in my way. Because of you, I cannot get close to other people. I expect too much from them and from myself. I cannot share in projects. I don't have fun because everything has to be done perfectly. Once you protected me from anxiety and fear, now you are a main source of my anxiety and fear. I want to feel "good enough" but you won't let me.*
> *I need to let you go.*

Sign your letter when you have finished it.

This is a letter that can be repeated several times with the same defense, or repeated with different defenses. Sometimes in doing this exercise you recognize that you aren't ready to let it go. If that is true, ask yourself what do you need to make it possible for you to let it go.

## IDENTIFYING FEELINGS

### EXERCISE 40

People often live in fear of their feelings. Hopefully, now that you are in a more protective environment and are exploring what various feelings mean to you, you'll begin to view feelings as a part of you to be listened to rather than feared. Allow feelings to be a part of you that gives you clues and signals. In this way, your feelings can evolve from a foe to a friend.

The first step in allowing your feelings to work for you is to begin to identify the feelings you experience in the course of a day. At the end of your day (on the checklist below), check off the feelings you experienced. After a few days of doing this, you will find yourself much more adept at being able to identify specific feelings.

| FEELINGS | MON | TUE | WED | THU | FRI | SAT | SUN |
|---|---|---|---|---|---|---|---|
| Angry | | | | | | | |
| Sad | | | | | | | |
| Guilty | | | | | | | |
| Lonely | | | | | | | |
| Embarrassed | | | | | | | |
| Happy | | | | | | | |
| Afraid | | | | | | | |
| Anxious | | | | | | | |
| Disappointed | | | | | | | |
| Hate | | | | | | | |
| Frustrated | | | | | | | |
| Disgusted | | | | | | | |
| Love | | | | | | | |
| Lust | | | | | | | |
| Compassionate | | | | | | | |
| Confident | | | | | | | |

| FEELINGS | MON | TUE | WED | THU | FRI | SAT | SUN |
|---|---|---|---|---|---|---|---|
| Jealous/Envious | | | | | | | |
| Affectionate | | | | | | | |
| Excited | | | | | | | |
| Bored | | | | | | | |
| Confused | | | | | | | |
| Numb | | | | | | | |
| Hurt | | | | | | | |
| Calm | | | | | | | |
| Secure | | | | | | | |
| Insecure | | | | | | | |
| Silly | | | | | | | |
| Playful | | | | | | | |

After a few days of working the above exercise, you will begin to recognize the specific feelings as you experience them. This next exercise is designed to work on the specific feelings that you are least able to identify. For instance, if you are working on identifying anger, stop yourself three times a day and write, "Today, up until this moment, I have been angry at . . ."

_____

_____

_____

_____

_____

_____

_____

If you are working on identifying fear, stop yourself three times a day and write, "Today, up until this moment, I have been afraid of . . ." (or "I have been afraid when . . ." or "I have been afraid that . . .")

_____

_____

_____

_____

After you've practiced this exercise to the extent that you can more easily identify these feelings, assign yourself the task of sharing them with someone else. Choose someone with whom you feel comfortable. Arrange to meet with this person on a regular basis. This could be a nightly telephone conversation, over lunch twice a week, or other similar arrangements. The purpose is not for your friend to problem-solve with you, but for you to practice and become more comfortable talking about your feelings.

Sometimes it is not in your best interest to express your feelings to the person toward whom you have those feelings. An example would be an employer who could feel threatened by your feelings and might retaliate. Your feelings in such cases are valid, and you don't need to hide or swallow them; you simply need to rely on other outlets to express them.

When you know that you feel a particular feeling and choose not to verbalize it, it's important to find another manner that will help you to express it.

Outlets for feelings—positive feelings of joy or happiness, as well as anger, sadness, or fear might be to:
1. Pound pillows
2. Run
3. Rip up newspapers
4. Write, journal
5. Play
6. Listen to music
7. Meditate

When feelings are externalized they become more tangible and less frightening. The process of beginning to fully experience feelings is often less than smooth. Some people go overboard in the discovery of their feelings and, for a time, talk about nothing else. Some people express their feelings in an exaggerated form, and are prone to be dramatic. As expressing your feelings becomes more natural to you, any need for them to be "bigger than life" will fade.

While no one acts on every feeling, it is usually wise to consider your feelings when making decisions. Anxiety might tell you that you need to change something in your life. Sadness might be a signal that you have suffered some kind of loss and perhaps need to mourn. More favorable emotions like joy and excitement might spur you toward decisions that help you find more of the same.

## GROUNDING: CIRCLE OF LIGHT

Sit comfortably in a chair—or lie down with a pillow under your head and another behind your knees.

Place one hand on your chest and another on your belly.

Take a very slow, very deep breath. As you count to yourself, about two numbers per second, draw air down toward your belly. Count up to six as you inhale. Breathe deeply enough for both the hand on your belly and the hand on your chest to move.

Let the breath out naturally.

Breathe in again very slowly, counting to six, feeling both hands rise. Release the breath and let it flow out.

Continue this deep breathing until you feel safe and relaxed.

If it feels safe, gently close your eyes; otherwise, lower your gaze.

With your next inhalation, imagine a large circle of healing light forming in front of you. This circle of light can be whatever size, shape, or color your imagination wants it to be.

When this circle of light is fully formed, picture yourself stepping into it and letting it slowly surround you.

With your next inhalation, breathe in as much of that healing light as you wish. Do this for several breaths.

Then, with each exhalation, let go of any tension in your body, and any worries, distress, or troubling thoughts in your head.

For a few minutes, continue to breathe in the healing light, and breathe out the tensions, worries, and distress.

If you like, you can end the activity here. Or you can go deeper, by imagining the healing light beginning to slowly massage your skin, starting with the top of your head, around the back and front of the face, then slowly making its way down and around your neck.

Continue to follow the light as it moves across the top of your shoulders and onto your shoulder blades. Stay with it as it slowly moves down your torso, and into and down your arms.

Let the healing light slowly continue to descend—all the way down your torso and arms, then into your hips and buttocks, and down into your hands. Follow the light as it spreads into your fingers and then out your fingertips, taking with it any tension from your body.

Feel the light continue to flow down through your legs, then around your ankles. Stay with the light as it flows into your feet, engulfing them.

As the healing light spreads down into your toes, and then out of them into the air, let the last of the tension in your body flow out with it.

Wiggle or shake your toes and fingers to get rid of any remaining stress.

Gently open your eyes and/or lift your gaze.

# CHAPTER THREE

# SELF-ESTEEM: FROM EXTERNAL RAGS TO INTERNAL RICHES

## SELF-ESTEEM OF FAMILY

### EXERCISE 41

To the outsider looking in, what occurs inside a home is frequently not as it appears. Families often portray a different reality to people outside of their family. Family members are often described as living behind masks.

Circle the words that best describe how other people perceived your family when you were a child. Then circle the words that portray what it was like for you from the inside.

| OTHER PEOPLE'S PERCEPTION | | HOW I SAW IT | |
|---|---|---|---|
| Happy | Caring | Happy | Caring |
| Loving | Quiet | Loving | Quiet |
| Warm | Loud | Warm | Loud |
| Safe | Scary | Safe | Scary |
| Insecure | Affectionate | Insecure | Affectionate |
| Angry | Violent | Angry | Violent |
| Hostile | Financially Secure | Hostile | Financially Secure |
| Distant | Financially Insecure | Distant | Financially Insecure |

## SELF-IMAGE

**EXERCISE 42**

When a child is raised in a family where everyone wears masks, that child usually grows into adulthood with his own mask.

Circle the words that you think reflect how other people perceive you now. Then circle the words you believe portray how you really are.

| OTHER PEOPLE'S PERCEPTIONS | | YOUR PERCEPTION | |
|---|---|---|---|
| Happy | Pretty | Happy | Pretty |
| Secure | Beautiful | Secure | Beautiful |
| Warm | Handsome | Warm | Handsome |
| Inadequate | Homely | Inadequate | Homely |
| Caring | Attractive | Caring | Attractive |
| Distant | Trim | Distant | Trim |
| Scared | Fat | Scared | Fat |
| Sad | Compassionate | Sad | Compassionate |
| Angry | Playful | Angry | Playful |
| Giving | Shy | Giving | Shy |
| Insecure | Confident | Insecure | Confident |
| Unhappy | Anxious | Unhappy | Anxious |
| Bright | Lonely | Bright | Lonely |
| Smart | Clumsy | Smart | Clumsy |
| Dumb | Graceful | Dumb | Graceful |
| Stupid | Talented | Stupid | Talented |
| Naive | | Naive | |

## LIKING YOURSELF

Acknowledging characteristics that you like about yourself is a positive and healthy quality. In unhealthy families, people generally don't like themselves. The acting-out person in such families usually has a great deal of self-hatred. Spouses experience self-doubt and self-blame. Not being able to like themselves, parents find it difficult to teach their children how to feel comfortable with and validate themselves.

Parents may ridicule you when they see you stand in front of the mirror. They may tease you about your weight, your walk, make derogatory comments such as, "So-and-so doesn't want to play with you because you're selfish, etc." These messages are internalized as *I'm not pretty. I walk funny. Being selfish is bad. I'm bad. Other people don't like me.*

Is it okay to feel good about yourself? Is it okay to compliment yourself? If you cannot say "yes" quickly and believe it in your heart, you need to look into why you hesitated or said "no."

Old messages about not being able to compliment yourself need to be countered with:
*It's okay to like myself, to compliment myself. Liking myself does not hurt anyone else.*

Add other positive messages that are relevant for you:

1. _____

_____

2. _____

_____

3. _____

_____

4. _____

_____

Sometimes we feel guilty when we feel good and others close to us feel badly, e.g. "I don't have the right to feel good, because Mom feels so bad all the time." Do you experience such guilt?

## SELF-VALUE

### EXERCISE 43

Name three things you value about yourself. They can be qualities or behaviors such as:

- I'm kind to animals.
- I'm a fast reader.
- I can solve Rubik's Cube.
- I am a caring person.

1. _____

2. _____

3. _____

Allow yourself to feel good about these traits or behaviors. Notice whether or not you begin to minimize or discount this self-affirmation. "Yes, but . . ." is the phrase that often begins a retraction. Speak slowly, pause between your different statements, and then pause again when you are finished. Pauses help to stop the negative message you may try to interject.

## NAME OF WORTH

### EXERCISE 44

Spell out your name. Now attach a positive attribute that starts with each letter and describes you.

Examples:

| | | |
|---|---|---|
| **R** risk taker | **S** skilled | **F** funny |
| **O** open-minded | **H** helpful | **R** religious |
| **B** brave | **E** eyes open | **A** animal lover |
| **E** energetic | **L** laughs | **N** neat |
| **R** responsible | **I** intelligent | **K** kind |
| **T** thinker | **A** assertive | **L** likeable |
| | | **I** interesting |
| | | **N** nice |

_____

_____

_____

_____

_____

_____

## ACCEPTING COMPLIMENTS

### EXERCISE 45

In healthy families, children are given sincere compliments regularly. In contrast, in dysfunctional families, compliments are often nonexistent, infrequent, or insincere—e.g. "Dad told me how much he liked me, but two hours later he asked me to lie for him." "While I received good grades at school, my parents never complimented me because they felt I should do well." In healthy families, compliments are accepted and believed. Children who didn't receive compliments, or had difficulty trusting them, have difficulty accepting compliments as adults. Inability to accept compliments leads to low self-esteem.

Think about compliments that you received when you were younger:

What did people compliment you for? _____

_____

_____

_____

Who complimented you? _____

_____

_____

_____

How did you feel, and what did you think when you were complimented? _____

_____

_____

_____

## JUST SAY THANKS

If you have difficulty receiving or accepting compliments, here is a plan that can help you be more receptive:

When you are complimented, pause for ten seconds. After the pause say "thank you." (Do this out of courtesy, if for no other reason.) Then, pause again for another ten seconds. This pausing allows you time to accept compliments—it disrupts any tendency you may have to reject it or say "yes, but . . ."

At first, receiving praise may feel awkward, but with practice it becomes more comfortable and more pleasurable.

## CRITICISM

### EXERCISE 46

People who have difficulty accepting compliments are often much more open to accepting criticism. As you listen to criticism be aware that you deserve to hear only constructive feedback. When criticized by whomever, ask yourself if you think there is validity to the feedback. If you are able to hear and accept what was said but don't know how to behave differently, don't hesitate to ask the person for suggestions.

People that grow up with chronic stress and trauma don't need others who are critical of them to make them feel bad—you become your own worst critic. Having internalized negative messages about yourself, you have an internal voice known as the inner critic. These messages are also shame-based beliefs that you come to internalize about yourself.

To quiet the harsh and negative aspects of your inner critic you must first be able to hear its words. If you are accustomed to it, it has become background noise that is ever-present yet unrecognized. The following exercise may help you to recognize the words of your critical self:

The trouble with me is  _____

The trouble with me is  _____

The trouble with me is  _____

I am just so _____

I am just so _____

I am just so _____

What I really don't like about myself is _____

What I really don't like about myself is _____

What I really don't like about myself is _____

- Where did those statements come from?
- Whose voices do you hear?
- How old were you when you began to believe it?
- With whom does the critic compare you?
- Where are its favorite places to rear its head—the bathroom scale, the mirror?
- What does your critic look like? How does it sound? What are its favorite noises or words?
- Would you be so harsh with someone else you cared for?
- Quieting your own inner critic is possible once you hear it.

With self-criticism, hear it, evaluate its validity, assess how you would respond differently next time, and move on. Don't sit in it.

# CRITICIZING OTHERS

## EXERCISE 47

Pick five people you most frequently come into contact with and rate them from (1) to (10). (1) being the least critical and (10) being constantly critical. Note with a number from (1) to (10) how frequently you are thinking or expressing critical thoughts of them. Then note what that criticism is about. The following sentence stems will help you identify the way people often start critical thinking:

- The trouble with you is . . .
- You are just so . . .
- What I really don't like about you is . . .

1. Name     _____

    (1)----------------------------------------(10)

    Least Critical            Most Critical

Frequency of my critical thoughts about them:    (1)----------------------------------------(10)

    Never            Very Frequent

2. Name     _____

    (1)----------------------------------------(10)

    Least Critical            Most Critical

Frequency of my critical thoughts about them:    (1)----------------------------------------(10)

    Never            Very Frequent

3. Name     _____

    (1)----------------------------------------(10)

    Least Critical            Most Critical

Frequency of my critical thoughts about them:    (1)----------------------------------------(10)

    Never            Very Frequent

4. Name     _____

    (1)----------------------------------------(10)

    Least Critical            Most Critical

Frequency of my critical thoughts about them:    (1)----------------------------------------(10)

    Never            Very Frequent

5. Name     _____

    (1)----------------------------------------(10)

    Least Critical            Most Critical

Frequency of my critical thoughts about them:    (1)----------------------------------------(10)

    Never            Very Frequent

Many times you develop not just critical thinking but an overall critical attitude. Picture yourself among a great number of people at a ballgame, on the freeway, or at a store. Using the same scale, note how critical of the general public you find yourself.

(1)----------------------------------------------------------------(10)

Never Critical                                           Very Frequent

## SHAMING MESSAGES

Shame is the painful feeling associated with the belief that who you are is not good enough, that you are inadequate, you are not worthy, and you are not of value. When you experience shame you feel defeated, alienated, never quite good enough to belong to your family, or even the human race. In the experience of shame there is also a sense of being exposed and vulnerable, of needing to hide your flaws or inadequate parts from yourself or others. You are not born with shame; it is something you learn, and you learn it from both family and culture.

### EXERCISE 48

1. Give examples of shaming messages you heard when growing up. *"You're stupid, dumb, ugly."*

_____

_____

_____

_____

2. Give examples of shaming behaviors you experienced. *Parents yelling at you in a public place; being made to stand in the corner for unrealistic periods of time.*

_____

_____

_____

_____

3. Give examples of shaming messages you received from parts of the wider culture—music, video, books and magazines, television, etc. *Your body has to be perfect. You're not a man if you don't have sexual conquests. You're not desirable to guys if you are too smart.*

_____

_____

_____

_____

4. How do you see those shaming messages/behaviors present in your life today? *Yelling at my own children in a public place; telling others they are stupid and incompetent; afraid of making a mistake; thinking others are smarter than I am; not trying things I'd like to do.*

_____

_____

_____

_____

## RECOVERY FROM SHAME ATTACKS

When you grow up in dysfunctional environments filled with shaming messages and behaviors, your ever-present, core belief is that you are flawed. So now when you are in stressful situations, or someone displays shaming behavior toward you or gives you a shaming message, you often experience what is called a Shame Attack. You feel like a young child again, defenseless, abandoned. You are terrified of this person or situation because it is recreating the trauma you experienced in your earlier environments. Shame Attacks incorporate all-or-nothing thinking. An example of a Shame Attack would be:

"I made a mistake in my finances and bounced a check. Since I bounced this check, I'll probably bounce many more, and I will have to declare bankruptcy, and then my credit will be ruined." From here, it's then very easy to start to shame yourself by saying, "I really am stupid and can't do anything right."

Another example of a Shame Attack would be: You are expected to present the culmination of a project at work tomorrow. You have worked diligently, but today you heard a co-worker's presentation and suddenly you know you will look unprepared and stupid. You immediately "catastrophize" the situation. "I will lose my job. "They will be sorry they hired me." And on and on and on.

## EXERCISE 49

If you are experiencing a Shame Attack, you need to:

- **Identify it for what it is.**

  *This is a Shame Attack.* I am feeling less than . . . and catastrophizing (only seeing the worst).

- **Stop the thinking.**

- **Objectify.**

  What is the reality here? Look at the previous two examples.

  **Check-bouncing Situation**

  *Reality:* You bounced a check. You made an error in your arithmetic. You were stressed and not thinking when you wrote the check.

  *Reality:* Most people at some time will bounce a check.

  *Reality:* You can call the source to which the check was made and tell them of your plan for repayment.

  **Fear of Presenting Work Project**

  *Reality:* You feel insecure. Another person made a good presentation. You have worked hard on this but are anxious. You want your superior to be impressed. None of this means you are incompetent. It says you are anxious. Past experience says your confidence shows once you begin your presentation.

- **Get outside feedback.**

  In a Shame Attack you are distorting the reality. You have lost sight of what is real, true . . . versus your fear.

- **Look at the origin of the shaming statement.**

  This is another important long-term tool in stopping a Shame Attack. After you've garnered a more realistic perspective, ask yourself: What were the harsh words I used against myself? They are usually words such as "I am stupid." "I can't do anything right." When did you first come to believe those things about yourself?

- Identify times you know you went into a shame attack and consider whether you could have talked yourself out of it if you had had this format to work with.

## STILTED SUCCESS

### EXERCISE 50

People often have difficulty recognizing or enjoying successes. You may be the person who accomplishes a goal and without a pause for reflection or celebration are immediately focused on the next goal. Or, by the time the goal is achieved you have managed to already discount your accomplishment. "I could have done it better, or more quickly."

To feel good about yourself, you must be able to acknowledge and enjoy your accomplishments. Reflect on what the word "success" means for you:

Success is _____

_____

_____

_____

_____

_____

_____

_____

### EXERCISE 51

The following exercise will help you ascertain whether your concept of success is connected to your past:

As a child, in order to succeed at home, I_____

_____

_____

As a child, in order to succeed at home, I_____

_____

_____

When I did accomplish something, _____

_____

_____

When I did accomplish something, _____

_____

_____

## GREAT EXPECTATIONS

Many times success (the accomplishment of a goal) is defined for children by their parent(s):

"You *must* go into the family business."

"You *must* attend college."

"You *must* achieve good grades in school."

"You *must* get a job in the medical field."

Success then becomes a *should*. When a goal is realized (e.g., graduation), there is no real elation because it was what you were *supposed* to do. Rather than a sense of accomplishment there is often a sense of emptiness. If you were raised to think in terms of what you *should* do then you can never truly enjoy your successes. Even when you excel, you lose, because it was really no big deal, and besides, there is the next goal to achieve.

Do you have difficulty enjoying your accomplishments because they are simply never good enough? No matter how well perceived by others, do you tend to discount the achievement because you think it could have been better? Many times, the phenomenon of "it wasn't good enough" comes from childhood experiences. Many children believed and hoped that if they were good enough or did something well enough, Mom might notice. Mom might say, "I love you." Dad might take you somewhere. Dad might quit drinking. Mom and Dad might quit fighting. Mom and Dad might get back together. The truth is that no matter how perfect you would have been, your behavior wasn't the reason your Mom and Dad were as they were. Yet today, as an adult, while you do not operate from the belief of "if I do this, Mom and Dad will do that," that belief that "it's not good enough" has still been internalized and become a way of life.

Another reason accomplishments are too often underappreciated is that before a project is even completed, another project often takes its place. For children, this happens as they manipulate their time in order to keep busy—to stay focused on tangible things in their lives and things they can control. Not having a project may have meant having time to relax, and relaxing meant "feeling," which was scary and threatening to survivorship. Not having a tangible project meant focusing on the intangible—the feelings, the drinking behavior, the fighting, the depressed behavior, and the other things you couldn't control.

## EXERCISE 52

Make a list of childhood accomplishments you experienced but did not really enjoy:

1. _____

_____

2. _____

_____

3. _____

_____

4. _____

_____

5. _____

_____

Now go back through your list, and note if you did not enjoy the experience because:
1.   It was a "should."
2.   It wasn't good enough.
3.   You immediately got involved in another project.

## EXERCISE 53

As an adult, what accomplishments have not been enjoyed because they were:

A "should":

1. _____

_____

2. _____

_____

Not good enough:

1. _____

_____

2. _____

_____

Moved to another project:

1. _____

_____

2. _____

_____

## ENJOYING SUCCESSES

Learning to be able to enjoy your successes (small or large) means:

- Pausing—taking the time—to enjoy them.
- Acknowledging that your behavior has value irrespective of the influence it has on someone else or their reactions.
- Basing your behavior and your expectations on what you genuinely want for yourself. This requires a lot of self-honesty. It also requires the ability to question and even to say "no" to other people's "shoulds." If you are imposing a lot of "shoulds" on yourself, stop to question them. Ask yourself, "Why should I?" "Who says so?" "Do I want to?" Try saying "no" to a few "shoulds," both yours and theirs. See how it feels.

## COGNITIVE DISTORITIONS WITH COUNTER-THOUGHT

Everyone engages in what is called cognitive distortions or faulty thinking to some degree. The following are examples of many forms of distorted thinking. They were most likely modeled for you and you continue to do what you were taught. The following table names and explains the distortion. Then it offers an example followed by an example of countering the faulty thinking.

| Distortion | | Negative Thought | Counter Thought |
|---|---|---|---|
| **All-or-Nothing Thinking** | You see things in black-and-white categories. | It's 8:30 A.M. and I'm late for work. I've spilled coffee on my new suit and put a run in my hosiery. This day is shot. | Good things may happen today. I can start my day over at any time. |
| **Overgeneralization** | You see a single negative event as a never-ending pattern of defeat. | Every time I drive on the freeway someone gets in my way and cuts me off. | There are lots of drivers who give me enough room. I'll focus on them instead of on the one who cut me off. |

| Distortion | | Negative Thought | Counter Thought |
|---|---|---|---|
| **Mental Filter** | You pick out a single negative detail and obsess on it so that your vision of all reality becomes darkened. | Every time I talk to my husband about my problems he tells me what to do. He's a bad husband. | At times my husband isn't the best listener, but he has other good qualities. |
| **Disqualifying the Positive** | You reject positive experiences by insisting they "don't count" for some reason or other. | Tiffany really liked my house but I know she was just being polite as her taste is so much better than mine. | Pause . . . take it in . . . that's nice that she said she liked my house. |
| **Jumping to Conclusions** | You make a negative interpretation even though there are no definite facts that convincingly support your conclusions. | She's late for dinner again and the food is getting cold. She's probably mad at me for being late to the movie last night. I'll bet she thinks I was late on purpose. | She's late for dinner again. I'm going to ask her when she gets here why she was late. |
| **Magnification/ Catastrophizing Or Minimization** | You exaggerate the importance of things or you inappropriately shrink things until they appear tiny. | The repairman didn't come on time and that means I'll be late to pick up the kids. Then dinner will be late. My husband will be mad and the kids will miss soccer practice. Sometimes I don't know why I bother. Life is so complicated and things don't work out the way they're supposed to. | This isn't the end of the world. If the repairman is more than fifteen minutes late, I'll call to reschedule. If the repair work takes too long, I'll ask my neighbor to pick up the kids. I can manage. |
| **Change Fallacy** | You believe that if another would just change their behavior your problems would go away. | If my mother would just work less, I know we would be closer to each other. | Whether my mother works less or more, only I can impact how I relate to her. |

| Distortion | | Negative Thought | Counter Thought |
|---|---|---|---|
| **Shoulds** | You try to motivate yourself or others with *should* and *shouldn't*. | I should not ever have to be angry if I just handle things right. | Everyone gets angry at times. I can learn to tolerate and express anger in a way that feels okay. |
| **Labeling & Mislabeling** | You attach a negative label to yourself. This is an extreme form of overgeneralization. | I am so stupid. I never should have volunteered to handle this project. I don't know what I'm doing. | Volunteering to do this project is scary. I may need some additional help. |
| **Personalization** | You see yourself as the cause of some negative external event. | My co-workers were laughing when they looked at me. I thought they were making fun of me. | I don't know why my co-workers were laughing; maybe they just heard a joke. |

## EXERCISE 54

Identify the two forms of distorted thinking that are most problematic for you.

1. _____

2. _____

For the next several weeks keep a daily journal and identify when you engage in either of your most problematic distortions, as in the table above, name the situation and your thought, and then offer a counter-thought. When you think you are stopping yourself, identify the next two cognitions you would like to work on and continue this process.

## ALL-OR-NOTHING PERSPECTIVE

This is one of the cognitive distortions presented in the previous exercise, but is included as a separate exercise as it is so prevalent. It is common to think in an all-or-nothing perspective—based on the belief that only one "right" and one "wrong" option exists. You are unable to consider other options. This extreme way of thinking about and viewing things causes a great deal of difficulty.

In this rigid thinking pattern there's no in-between. When you choose to trust someone, you are totally trusting, revealing all your vulnerabilities or, if you are distrustful, you reveal no information about yourself. You are either unfeeling or overcome with feelings, or experience being very needy of others to believing you need no one. You swing from one extreme to the other. You might bounce from feeling "in control" to feeling "out of control," or from feeling great to feeling despair.

This kind of all-or-nothing behavior may have been modeled for you growing up. For example, "My mother was either very nice to us or she totally ignored us." "My father was a very loving, giving person when he was sober, but when he was drunk, he was very mean, very violent, or he simply was absent."

## EXERCISE 55

Was all-or-nothing behavior modeled for you growing up? If so, what form did it take?

_____

_____

_____

_____

_____

_____

_____

## EXERCISE 56

All-or-nothing thinking also stems from childhood beliefs that, "If I do one thing wrong in my life, I might as well not bother trying to do anything right," or "I must do it this way (there are no alternatives) or something very bad will happen."

Fears that often contribute to such extreme ways of thinking include, "I have to do 'such-and-such' or my mom/dad won't love me." "I have to do 'such-and-such' or I'll cry/get angry and then something worse will happen." "If I don't do 'such-and-such' my friends will make fun of me or others will know what is really happening."

Reflecting on your early years, consider what thoughts and fears you experienced that may have contributed to your all-or-nothing thinking:

As a child . . .

1.  I _____

or (would happen) _____

2.  I _____

or (would happen) _____

3.  I _____

or (would happen) _____

4.  I _____

or (would happen) _____

5.  I _____

or (would happen) _____

It is important to view things as part of a process as an alternative to all-or-nothing or "either/or" thinking. All-or-nothing thinking is unnecessarily rigid and often leads to feeling "crazy" as you bounce from one extreme to the other. Examples of such thinking are:

"If I don't get to the dinner party it will be a disaster."

**Alternative thought**: "If I don't get to the dinner party, I will be disappointed, as will others. But the food will still get put on the table, and people will eat."

"If I don't finish this by today, I'll totally mess up tomorrow's schedule."

**Alternative thought**: "If this doesn't get done today, I'll have to rearrange tomorrow morning's schedule. By the end of the week, everything on the schedule will have been addressed."

## EXERCISE 57

List situations where you have a tendency to view things in extremes or as all-or-nothing:

1. _____

_____

2. _____

_____

3. _____

_____

4. _____

_____

Acting on these extreme views typically means moving in leaps and bounds rather than taking progressive steps. Modifying all-or-nothing behavior means developing the ability to be in greater balance.

For example, if your anger is all-or-nothing, a balance point between "being fine" and "rage" is "frustration." If trust is an either/or issue for you, a place of balance would be to be able to trust some people with some information, but not other information. If your need for people is an all-or-nothing issue, balance may be the understanding that "I have needs, some of which are more important to me now than others; some need to incorporate other people, and some do not." Go back to your list of all-or-nothing issues and identify an example of balanced thinking that demonstrates greater flexibility.

On a daily basis, reflect back at the end of each day on any all-or-nothing thinking, attitudes, or behaviors you experienced. Identify other options and alternative thoughts. While hindsight may not correct the past situation, the act of learning to identify rigid thoughts and developing alternative perceptions will help you to begin to see options as they arise. You will soon see yourself becoming much more flexible.

## PRESENT-DAY SELF-ESTEEM

As a child, you may have internalized a great deal of self-doubt, powerlessness, and shame. You may have grown up in a home where you were not given consistent nurturing and validation. Praise and positive attention may have been guilt motivated, or inconsistent or simply absent. While some children are more or less ignored in terms of their basic needs for nurturing, others are frequently verbally discounted and berated.

Whatever the sources of feeling poorly about yourself are, it is now time to change that way of thinking. A greater sense of self-esteem will emerge as you begin to believe in yourself.

Three times a day, for two weeks, stop yourself and identify something you have done or said that is a sign of your healing and recovery, or simply a positive reflection of you. The smallest and seemingly insignificant affirmation is acceptable as long as it is nice, considerate, or of value to you.

For example:

> "I took time to exercise."
> "I called a friend I hadn't talked to in a long time."
> "I didn't do a co-worker's work."
> "I honked my horn in traffic (vs. keeping my anger in)."
> "I spoke up in my group therapy session."

Keep a notebook to be able to reflect back. Continue this exercise until self-praise and feeling good become automatic. Periodically repeat this assignment to keep these skills in practice.

Don't "yes, but . . . " yourself. Oftentimes in the beginning, you might want to discount yourself by saying, "I was honest, but not in every situation." "I said no, but I could have said it more today." You aren't striving for perfection. Don't focus on the parts of yourself that you don't like. Concentrate and acknowledge the parts of yourself that are part of your process of recovery and healing.

While you need to actively participate in the strengthening of your self-esteem, know that associating with supportive nurturing people is also a sign of positive self-regard that supports your self-esteem. As I wrote in *The Truth Begins with You:* **"Surround yourself with people who respect and treat you well."**

## ROLES

Children raised in dysfunctional homes typically play one or more roles within the family structure. While these roles were part of your survival mechanism, they were also the way you garnered attention and/or felt good about yourself.

These roles are: The Responsible Child (Hero), The Placater, The Adjuster (Lost Child), Mascot, and the Acting-Out Child (Scapegoat). People usually identify with at least two of these roles. Many identify with two or three at the same time in their lives, while others identify with one role for a while and then clearly switch to a second role. Unfortunately, because these roles are rigidly adopted so children can emotionally survive their experiences growing up, there are invariably negative consequences. Most people easily recognize strengths in the first three roles, but not the downsides of each. It will be important to identify the role you adopted for survival in your family, as well as the parts of that identity you'd like to keep and the parts you'd like to give up now that you are an adult.

## THE RESPONSIBLE CHILD

### EXERCISE 58

The responsible child, otherwise known as the "nine-year-old going on thirty-five," tends to be organized and goal-oriented. The responsible child is adept at planning and manipulating others to get things accomplished, allowing him to be in a leadership position. He is often independent and self-reliant, capable of accomplishments and achievements.

But, because these accomplishments are made less out of conscious choice than out of a necessity to survive (emotionally, if not physically), there is a price paid for this "early maturity." For example, "As a result of being the 'little adult' in my family, I didn't have time to play baseball because I had to make dinner for my sisters."

Complete the following:

As a result of being the little adult, I didn't have time to _____

_____

because _____

_____

As a result of being the little adult, I didn't have time to _____

_____

because _____

_____

As a result of being the little adult, I didn't have time to _____

_____

because _____

_____

As a result of being the little adult, I didn't have time to _____

_____

because _____

_____

## THE PLACATING CHILD

### EXERCISE 59

The placater, otherwise known as the "household social worker" or "caretaker," is the child who takes care of everyone else's emotional needs. This is the young girl who perceives her sister's embarrassment when Mom shows up at a school open house drunk and will do whatever is necessary to take the embarrassment away. This is the boy comforting his brother in the face of his disappointment in Dad's absence at a ball game. This is the child who intervenes to calm his frightened siblings after a screaming match between their parents. This is a warm, sensitive, listening, caring person who shows a tremendous capacity to help others feel better.

For the placater, emotional survival is about giving one's time, energy, and empathy to take away the fears, sadness, and guilt of others. But as adults, people who have spent years taking care of others often pay a heavy price for this "imbalance of focus." For example, "As a result of being the 'household social worker,' I didn't have time for myself. I never talked to anyone about *my* problems because I was too busy taking care of my siblings and being involved in solving their problems."

Complete the following:

As a result of being the household social worker, I didn't have time to _____

_____

because _____

_____

As a result of being the household social worker, I didn't have time to _____

_____

because _____

_____

As a result of being the household social worker, I didn't have time to _____

_____

because _____

_____

As a result of being the household social worker, I didn't have time to _____

_____

because _____

_____

## THE ADJUSTING CHILD

### EXERCISE 60

The adjusting child finds it easier to go along with whatever is happening in the family, no matter how chaotic and unhealthy it might be. Adjusters do not question, think about, or respond directly to what was occurring in their life. They simply "adjust" to what they experience, often by detaching themselves emotionally, physically, and socially as much as is possible.

While it is easier to survive the frequent confusion and hurt of a dysfunctional home through adjusting, there are many negative consequences for the adjusters in adult life. For example, "As a result of adjusting/detaching I got into a lot of strange situations because I didn't stop to think or do anything different."

Complete the following:

As a result of adjusting/detaching I_____

_____

because _____

_____

As a result of adjusting/detaching I_____

_____

because _____

_____

As a result of adjusting/detaching I_____

_____

because _____

_____

As a result of adjusting/detaching I_____

_____

because _____

_____

# THE MASCOT CHILD

## EXERCISE 61

The mascot is the person who is often perceived as the family pet; he or she most likely uses charm and humor to distract from situations that are painful, as well as it often being the one way he or she can garner some positive attention.

Complete the following:

As a result of being the mascot, I didn't have the chance to _____

_____

because _____

_____

As a result of being the mascot, I didn't have the chance to _____

_____

because _____

_____

As a result of being the mascot, I didn't have the chance to _____

_____

because _____

_____

As a result of being the mascot, I didn't have the chance to _____

_____

because _____

_____

## THE ACTING-OUT CHILD

### EXERCISE 62

Some kids in unhealthy homes become angry and rebellious at a young age. They are confused and scared, and act out their confusion in ways that get them a lot of negative attention. As a result, they get into trouble at home, school and, often, on the streets. Through their behavior, these kids are screaming, "There's something wrong here!" The negative consequences of taking on the role of the acting-out child are more obvious than in the other three roles. For example, "Because of my acting-out behavior, I was suspended from school many times."

Complete the following:

As a result of my acting-out behavior, I didn't have time to _____

_____

_____

As a result of my acting-out behavior, I didn't have time to _____

_____

_____

As a result of my acting-out behavior, I didn't have time to _____

_____

_____

As a result of my acting-out behavior, I didn't have time to _____

_____

_____

# ADULT ROLES

## EXERCISE 63

Today as an adult I am still (check the appropriate boxes):

☐ Overly responsible

☐ Placating

☐ Adjusting

☐ Being the mascot

☐ Acting-out negatively

As a result, I still haven't learned _____

_____

_____

_____

_____

_____

It is important for me to take the time to (be specific) _____

_____

_____

_____

_____

Remember, you don't have to give up the positive things you learned in the roles you took on in your original family. Balance and moderation is the goal. As the responsible child, you don't have to give up your ability to lead and take charge, but you can allow others the opportunity so that you can have a break. As a placater, you may retain your sensitivity to situations, but no longer at your expense. As an adjuster, you can utilize your flexibility and adaptability, while trusting your own ability to make decisions. As a mascot, you can retain a sense of humor, while also being willing to focus on the moment. As an acting-out adult child, you don't have to give up your anger, but you can modify it, asking for what you need and want in a more calm, direct manner.

## FEMININE/MASCULINE

Feeling positive about your feminine/masculine aspects is an important element in liking and embracing yourself. You may feel secure and comfortable in your maleness and femaleness; you may recognize that you like some things that are attributed to your gender and feel hampered by others. Then again, you may feel insecure. These exercises will help you explore those values you attribute to being male or female.

## BEING FEMININE

### EXERCISE 64

Complete the following, whether you are male or female.

Being a girl in my family meant _____

_____

_____

Being a girl in my family meant _____

_____

_____

Being a girl in my family meant _____

_____

_____

Being the (circle one) only, first, second, third, ( _____ ) girl in my family meant _____

_____

_____

## EXERCISE 65

My mom's femininity was something I (circle one)          liked          disliked

| **What I liked** | **What I disliked** |
|---|---|
| _____ | _____ |
| _____ | _____ |
| _____ | _____ |
| _____ | _____ |
| _____ | _____ |

(For the female reader)

Today, as an adult, being female means _____

_____

_____

_____

_____

_____

_____

_____

_____

_____

## BEING MASCULINE

### EXERCISE 66

Complete the following whether you are male or female.

Being a boy in my family meant _____

_____

_____

Being a boy in my family meant _____

_____

_____

Being a boy in my family meant _____

_____

_____

Being the only, first, second, third, _____ (circle one) boy in my family meant _____

_____

_____

## EXERCISE 67

My dad's masculinity was something I (circle one)          liked          disliked

| **What I liked** | **What I disliked** |
| --- | --- |
| _____ | _____ |
| _____ | _____ |
| _____ | _____ |
| _____ | _____ |
| _____ | _____ |

(For the male reader)

Today, as an adult, being male means _____

_____

_____

_____

_____

_____

_____

_____

_____

_____

## EXERCISE 68

How does your familial experience regarding messages about being male or female influence you today? How does it affect how you feel about yourself? In what ways does it affect your relationships with others of your own and the opposite gender?

_____

_____

_____

_____

_____

_____

_____

_____

_____

_____

**Before you move on to explore other parts of yourself, let me say that while there are stereotyped messages of being male/female, masculine/feminine, feelings and abilities are not exclusive to any one gender.**

# AFFIRMATIONS

Affirmations are positive self-talk; they can be used to counter negative self-statements.

If you struggle with engaging in affirmations as it may seem silly and childlike, there is science to the validity of using them. There are three main psychological explanations for why self-affirmation is beneficial: First, it's simply enjoyable to dwell on what you value; second, when you're feeling threatened by a particular criticism or failure, the technique reminds you of those things you value about yourself more broadly, that are separate from the threatened aspect; third, by broadening the basis of your self-worth, it can help you regulate your emotions. It is recommended you practice these daily for at least ninety days for it to become a habit that is incorporated into your day with ease.

## EXERCISE 69
**Guidelines for an affirmation**:

- Make it short and simple: "I am a creative person."
- Use the present tense: "I am . . ."
- Avoid negative phraseology; instead of saying, "I am no longer afraid to assert myself," try, "I am assertive."

A helpful way to start the affirmation process is to make a declaration of a positive change that you want to make. A declarative statement could start with:

"I am learning . . ."          "I am willing to . . ."

"I am discovering . . ."          "I am becoming . . ."

**Examples of positive change**:

"I am learning to say no."

"I am willing to set limits."

"I am discovering I am courageous."

"I am becoming confident and secure."

**More definitive affirmations would be**:

"I am a unique and capable person just as I am."

"I am deserving of good things in my life."

"I take responsibility for me."

"I am setting limits for myself."

Identify three affirmations that you are willing to practice.

1. _____

2. _____

3. _____

Two primary methods of reinforcing an affirmation—or any new pattern of thinking—are repetition and feeling. Choose a setting and time of day during which you are most relaxed, and then say the affirmation slowly, with feeling and a sense of conviction. Repeat it a second time, just as slowly, with feeling and conviction. Repeat it a third, fourth, and fifth time.

Writing down your affirmations and having them accessible to read is helpful in reminding you of your strengths. You might carry them in your pocket, purse, or wallet, or post them in notes on your cell phone, on your computer, bathroom mirror, refrigerator, etc.

## GROUNDING: HEALING COLORS

Sit comfortably on a cushion or the front of a chair with your back straight but not stiff. Breathe slowly and deeply for a minute or two.

Close your eyes. Take a few more deep breaths.

Imagine a place of beauty and safety. This might be the bank of a river or a sun-drenched beach or the deck of a sailboat in calm water or your favorite chair in your living room or a spot in your backyard or garden.

Now envision yourself in that spot. If you are outdoors, imagine a light breeze in your face; if you are indoors, imagine a gorgeous view out a nearby window.

If you like, you can be alone in this mental place. Or if you prefer, one or more people whom you feel safe with can be there with you.

As you continue to breathe deeply, imagine colors are starting to appear around you. These are colors of love, of nurturing, of safety. Don't try to create any particular colors; let them emerge naturally. They may be blues and purples, oranges and reds, or yellows and greens. Whatever colors help you feel safe and relaxed, let them arise and fill the space around you.

Stay in this place of safety and beauty for as long as you like. Know that you can come back to this place at any time you choose.

# CHAPTER FOUR

# CREATING A STRONGER SENSE OF SELF

## NEEDING PEOPLE

It is through connecting with others that you so often find meaning in life. When your interpersonal needs as a child were not met, you came to discount your needs for people today, or experienced the other extreme of feeling an insatiable need for others.

### EXERCISE 70

Many times adults are unavailable when children need them. A child may need a kind word, a hug, help in solving a problem, or validation. In problematic families, these things usually either don't happen or happen only inconsistently.

How much might a kind word, a hug, help with solving a problem have helped:

- When you struggled with poor grades at school
- When a schoolmate bullied you
- When you were home sick
- When you brought home an "A" from school
- When you excelled in soccer
- When a family member or friend berated you.

Think about situations that occurred in which you wanted a person in your life to respond and to make themselves available to you, and they did not. Note the person (mother, father, grandparent, brother, sister, friend, teacher, lover, spouse, friend) and the occasion:

**Ages**

Before 6     1. _____

                  _____

             2. _____

                  _____

6–11         1. _____

                  _____

             2. _____

                  _____

12–17        1. _____

                  _____

             2. _____

                  _____

18–24        1. _____

                  _____

             2. _____

                  _____

25–34        1. _____

                  _____

             2. _____

                  _____

35–44        1. _____

                  _____

2. _____

_____

45–54        1. _____

_____

2. _____

_____

55–64        1. _____

_____

2. _____

_____

65 +         1. _____

_____

2. _____

_____

## EXERCISE 71

It is just as important to recognize when people have been available when you needed them, as it is to identify when they have not. List those situations and the person who did respond and made him- or herself available to you.

### Ages

Before 6     1. _____

_____

2. _____

_____

6–11    1. _____

       _____

       2. _____

       _____

12–17    1. _____

       _____

       2. _____

       _____

18–24    1. _____

       _____

       2. _____

       _____

25–34    1. _____

       _____

       2. _____

       _____

35–44    1. _____

       _____

       2. _____

       _____

45–54    1. _____

       _____

2. _____

_____

55–64     1. _____

_____

2. _____

_____

65 +     1. _____

_____

2. _____

_____

Put a star (★) by the names of people mentioned above who you could trust to be available to you today.

## PETS

Pets often become very significant in the lives of children whose needs aren't being met by people. A pet can be a friend who listens to whatever a child (or an adult) has to say without offering judgment. Pets love those who care for them unconditionally. Many times pets can be held, and sometimes they lick the tears from our faces. They are often warm and cuddly.

### EXERCISE 72

What animals did you have as you were growing up? Were they family pets, or your pets specifically? List all of your pets from childhood to the today, and describe your relationship with them:

_____

_____

_____

_____

_____

_____

_____

_____

_____

_____

_____

_____

_____

## "NEEDS" LETTER

### EXERCISE 73

The following exercise is to assist you in identifying your needs. Write a letter to each of your parents, including stepparents. *These letters are for your understanding, not theirs—they are not meant to be sent.* Spend approximately twenty–thirty minutes on each, and write no more than three pages per letter. Allow yourself at least one week between the writing of each letter.

The purpose for doing these letters is:

1.   It is often cathartic, and moves you one more step through the grief process.
2.   To recognize that there are things to be grateful for.
3.   It aids in recognizing your childhood needs.
4.   As a result of recognizing childhood needs, it is often easier to identify adult needs, making it more likely that you can now go about getting those needs met.

Begin by writing:

*Dear Mom (or Dad),*

Thank your parent for what he or she gave you, e.g., "I want to thank you Mom for always remembering my birthdays and making them special." "Thank you for encouraging me to play the piano. I still play. Thanks for coming to my school play in the second grade. Thanks for letting me go to my girlfriend's house on nights when Dad was real bad."

Obviously, you could say something like, "Hey, Mom, where were you during my other school plays?" "Why didn't you leave Dad?" "Why didn't you ever play with me?" But pass on that now, and sincerely thank your parent for a few things that they did give you.

Then (after a maximum of six or seven "thank yous"), tell this parent what it is you needed from him or her that you didn't get. "I needed you to protect me from Dad." "I needed you to tell me it was okay for me to be angry." "I needed you to come into the bedroom and notice when I was crying. You never came in." "I needed you to follow through on your promises." This is a much lengthier part of the letter.

If you have difficulty saying thank you, you may want to do the second part of the letter first. Undoubtedly, for some people, what they have to be thankful for may be very small; that's okay. Sign your letter when you have finished it.

After your letter is completed, circle the needs you expressed and ask yourself if they are still needs today. Needs such as "I needed to play," and/or "I needed to be able to make mistakes and not feel I was a bad person," are typically carried to adulthood. While those needs are not going to be met by a parent, you can take responsibility for and find ways of meeting them today.

## I HAVE NEEDS

### EXERCISE 74

Indicate where you are on a scale from 1–10: 10 means you do it well and consistently, 1 means it is not a part of your life. If you mark below 7, what's getting in the way? If it has been difficult in your life, at what age did you give it up?

Ability or willingness:

to play          1------------------------10

to laugh         1------------------------10

to relax                                                1----------------------10

to be flexible                                          1----------------------10

to lead yet also feel comfortable following             1----------------------10

to question                                             1----------------------10

to talk honestly                                        1----------------------10

to make decisions                                       1----------------------10

to attend to my own needs                               1----------------------10

to recognize where my power lies                        1----------------------10

to protect myself                                       1----------------------10

to know and accept my feelings                          1----------------------10

to be able to express those feelings                    1----------------------10

to no longer live life in fear                          1----------------------10

to believe in my specialness                            1----------------------10

to ask for help                                         1----------------------10

to make time for self                                   1----------------------10

to make time for others                                 1----------------------10

to experience appropriate touch                         1----------------------10

to be able to set limits                                1----------------------10

to exercise                                             1----------------------10

to practice spirituality                                1----------------------10

Other: _____                1----------------------10

Other: _____                1----------------------10

Other: _____                1----------------------10

# BOUNDARIES

For children raised in troubled families, boundaries are rarely respected and sometimes nonexistent. You may have lived with rigid, walled boundaries, offering no opportunity for any emotional or spiritual connection. Unhealthy boundaries create confusion about who is responsible for what, adding more distortion about guilt and shame. As a consequence of growing up in a family where boundaries are unhealthy, adults are unaware of how to set boundaries for themselves, and are often disrespectful and intrusive with regard to the boundaries of others.

A boundary is a limit or edge that defines where one person and their rights end and another person and their rights begin. Your boundaries delineate you as a separate human being, rather than as part of someone else. While your skin marks the limit of the physical self, everyone has other boundaries as well—emotional, spiritual, sexual, relationship, and intellectual boundaries. Emotional boundaries define feelings and values. You set emotional boundaries by choosing how you let people treat you. Your spiritual development comes from your inner self. Only you truly know your spiritual path. Sexual boundaries are limits on what you define as safe and appropriate sexual behavior. You have choices about who you interact with sexually and the extent of that interaction. Relationship boundaries define the limits of appropriate interaction with others. Intellectual boundaries guide learning, curiosity, interests, and thinking.

## EXERCISE 75

Circle the number that best describes the boundaries in the family in which you were raised:

1. No boundaries
2. Damaged boundaries
3. Walled boundaries—walls of anger, fear, silence, words
4. Healthy boundaries

Describe the unhealthy boundaries you witnessed or experienced:

_____

_____

_____

Describe healthy boundaries you witnessed or experienced:

_____

_____

_____

## "NO" AND "YES"

To be able to have healthy boundaries, it is important to be able to say "no" and "yes" freely.

### EXERCISE 76

Establishing and maintaining appropriate boundaries requires being able to say, "No." Without the ability to say no, you easily become overextended and end up feeling victimized and used. More importantly, saying no is vital to assuring your needs are met. If you cannot say no, you'll never know if you're saying yes freely.

Complete the following sentences about what happens when you say, "No":

Examples may be, "When I say no, I am afraid that people won't like me." "When I say no, I sound like my mother."

When I say no, I _____

_____

_____

When I say no, I _____

_____

_____

When I say no, I _____

_____

_____

Summarize what beliefs interfere with your ability to say no:

_____

_____

_____

_____

# "NO"

## EXERCISE 77

How did your mom say no? Did she scream, "No! You can't!" or did she say *yes* at first, and then sabotage the situation so it became a no? Did she ever say no? Was she fair?

Write about your experience hearing "no" from your mom:

_____

_____

_____

_____

_____

_____

_____

_____

Note helpful "no's" you heard: _____

_____

_____

Note hurtful "no's" you heard: _____

_____

_____

## EXERCISE 78

How did your dad say no? Did he scream, "No! You can't!" or did he say *yes* at first and then sabotage the situation so it became a no? Did he ever say no? Was he fair?

Write about hearing "no" from your dad:

_____

_____

_____

_____

_____

_____

_____

_____

Note helpful "no's" you heard: _____

_____

_____

Note hurtful "no's" you heard: _____

_____

_____

## EXERCISE 79

Describe other "no's" you heard when you were younger (e.g., when your application to a particular school was turned down, or a prospective date declined to go out with you, or how you tried out for a team and didn't make it).

_____

_____

_____

## EXERCISE 80

Reflecting on all of this, does the ability to say no interfere with your life today? If so, describe what beliefs come up for you when others say "no" to you:

_____

_____

_____

_____

_____

## "YES"

### EXERCISE 81

For people who have difficulty saying "no" examining what the word "yes" means is helpful in that yes and no are part of the same continuum. Some people have little or no difficulty saying no while yes causes much internal conflict. For greater insight, complete the following sentences:

When I say yes, I _____

_____

_____

When I say yes, I _____

_____

_____

When I say yes, I _____

_____

_____

Summarize what beliefs interfere with your ability to say yes:

_____

_____

_____

_____

_____

_____

## EXERCISE 82

How did your mom say "yes"? Did she say yes only by never saying a clear "no"? Did she always have to get an answer from your father? Did she say yes to everything?

Write about hearing "yes" from your mom:

_____

_____

_____

_____

_____

_____

_____

_____

Note helpful "yes's" you heard: _____

_____

_____

Note hurtful "yes's" you heard: _____

_____

_____

**EXERCISE 83**

How did your dad say "yes"? Did he always say yes? Did he tend to say yes, but attach a warning? Was he fair?

Write about hearing "yes" from your dad:

_____

_____

_____

_____

_____

_____

_____

Note helpful "yes's" you heard: _____

_____

_____

Note hurtful "yes's" you heard: _____

_____

_____

**EXERCISE 84**

Describe other "yes's" you've heard when you were younger:

_____

_____

_____

Reflecting on all of this, does the ability to say yes interfere with your life today? If so, describe what beliefs come up for you when others say "yes" to you:

_____

_____

_____

_____

_____

_____

_____

## PRACTICING "NO" AND "YES"

Now that you have an understanding of what the words "no" and "yes" mean, you may discover that you'd like to be able to use either word more frequently *and* feel good about it. Practice saying the word "no" in front of a mirror. Say it loud. Louder. Louder. Practice saying the word "yes" in front of a mirror. Say it loud. Louder. Louder.

It's important to practice saying them so that when you need to say them in real life, you can do so more naturally and comfortably. Don't just practice prior to knowing that you want to use it. Practice it now so that you'll have the ability to use it any time you need to. View these words as a part of you, just as feelings are a part of you. They're to be your friend, not your foe.

**EXERCISE 85**

If "no" is difficult for you to say, complete the following sentences:

It is okay to say no. When I say no I will feel better about myself because_____

_____

_____

It is okay to say no. When I say no I will feel better about myself because_____

_____

_____

It is okay to say no. When I say no I will feel better about myself because_____

_____

_____

Only after you have come to an understanding of what "no" has meant in your life, become comfortable with verbalizing the word, and believe in the value of it, will you begin to apply the words "yes" and "no" appropriately.

**EXERCISE 86**

List four situations in which you would like to say "no" (e.g., when you are asked to go to a restaurant you aren't fond of, or when you are asked to work during your lunch time), and prioritize them in order of difficulty for you: #1 being the easiest to do, #4 being the most difficult for you to do. Do this on a weekly basis, and begin saying no to the less difficult situations.

1. _____

_____

2. _____

_____

3. _____

_____

4. _____

_____

## EXERCISE 87

If "yes" is difficult for you to say, complete the following sentences:

It is okay to say yes. When I say yes I will feel better about myself because _____

_____

_____

It is okay to say yes. When I say yes I will feel better about myself because _____

_____

_____

It is okay to say yes. When I say yes I will feel better about myself because _____

_____

_____

## EXERCISE 88

List four situations in which you would like to say yes (e.g., when you are asked to go to a party, or when you are asked to join a group), and prioritize them in order of difficulty for you: #1 being the easiest to do, #4 being the most difficult for you to do. Do this on a weekly basis, and begin saying yes to the less difficult situations.

1. _____

_____

2. _____

_____

3. _____

_____

4. _____

_____

## INAPPROPRIATE BEHAVIOR

Tolerance for inappropriate behavior is developed when people have been subjected to situations such as lying, drunkenness, verbal abuse, privacy not being respected, etc. The most common response to this is to take on a victim stance in life. High tolerance leads to denial and the inability to recognize inappropriate and hurtful behavior. The troubled family rules—*Don't Talk, Don't Trust, Don't Feel, Don't Think*, and *Don't Question*—fuel this ongoing tolerance.

### EXERCISE 89

List examples of situations you experienced as a child and/or adolescent in which someone else's behavior was inappropriate or hurtful, and yet no one said anything. You might identify such situations by asking yourself, "Was it crazy or hurtful behavior, and everyone acted as if it wasn't happening?" List four examples:

1. _____

_____

2. _____

_____

3. _____

_____

4. _____

_____

## EXERCISE 90

If you developed a high tolerance for inappropriate or hurtful behavior by virtue of what you were exposed to as a child, you are likely continuing that pattern today.

List examples of situations you have experienced as an adult in which someone's behavior was inappropriate/hurtful and you didn't say anything:

1. _____

_____

2. _____

_____

3. _____

_____

4. _____

_____

## INTRUSIVE BEHAVIOR

### EXERCISE 91

Some people haven't learned a healthy respect for other people's boundaries. It is difficult for intrusive people to self-identify intrusive behavior. Ask yourself these questions: "Do I intrude on other people?" "Am I inconsiderate, and therefore rude?"

Some people blatantly intrude, such as inviting themselves to spend the night; others intrude in more passive ways, e.g., attempting to relieve another person of unpleasant feelings before that person has had a chance to verbalize them. Under the guise of caring and wanting to help someone, helpers can be intrusive, particularly if the motivation for caring is to be noticed or to receive approval.

Identifying intrusive behavior in others makes it easier to recognize your own intrusive behavior.

Examples:

- When you wanted privacy while bathing, your mother insisted on being able to enter the bathroom at any time.
- A sister took your toys to her room without asking and didn't return them.
- Dad would walk in and change the television station even though the kids were engrossed in a show.

List examples of intrusive behavior that took place in your family:

1. _____

_____

2. _____

_____

3. _____

_____

4. _____

_____

As you identify inappropriate behavior, you are learning to identify the "intruding" person.

## EXERCISE 92

Name three people with whom you (as an adult) frequently find yourself having to say no to or with whom you must set limits:

1. _____

_____

2. _____

_____

3. _____

_____

You could rationalize that these three people have an amazing capacity to ask for or perhaps simply take what they need, but perhaps they are just highly intrusive. You can ask for what you need without being intrusive. No one likes hearing "no" when they want something, but a healthy person will respect your needs and wishes. Intrusive people push for their needs without recognizing or caring about the needs or rights of others.

You may have practiced intrusive behavior in your adulthood. If you are intrusive, you may not be aware of this behavior. You may have an attitude that incorporates communal ownership: "This is my house, and I can do what I want, when I want." "Being family, they won't mind." "They have a lot of time, so it will be okay." Intrusive people make generalized assumptions that help to justify their behavior and assure they get what they want.

If you identify with these previous attitudes and are questioning whether or not you are intrusive, you may need to seek the feedback of a close friend. Ask your friend to help you identify those instances when you were intrusive and made assumptions about their time or their belongings.

## EXERCISE 93

List four examples of your intrusive experiences:

1. _____

_____

2. _____

_____

3. _____

_____

4. _____

_____

If you identify with a high tolerance for inappropriate behavior, have difficulty knowing what appropriate behavior is, or find yourself being intrusive to others, then the key to stopping this behavior is learning to question. When you find yourself in an uncomfortable situation—STOP, and pause. Ask yourself the following questions: *Is this behavior okay with me? Are my feelings being respected? Am I being respectful of their feelings and time?* Before you can answer these questions honestly, you'll have to be able to identify feelings and feel a sense of your own worth.

## BOUNDARY VIOLATIONS FROM BOTH SIDES OF THE CONTINUUM

This exercise is another way in which to identify boundary violations you have experienced on the part of others or engage in yourself.

## EXERCISE 94

Place a check ☑ on the left for boundary violations you have experienced.
Place a check ☑ on the right for boundary violations that you have enacted on others.

**Physical:**

- ☐ accepting touch you do not want ☐
- ☐ not taught appropriate hygiene ☐
- ☐ violence, pushing, shoving, kicking, pinching ☐
- ☐ excessive tickling, hitting ☐
- ☐ touch deprivation ☐
- ☐ not allowing a person to have privacy ☐
- ☐ going into a person's belongings or living space without permission ☐
- ☐ exposing someone to illness ☐

**Sexual:**

- ☐ being sexual for partner, not self ☐
- ☐ lack of sexual information during puberty ☐
- ☐ given misinformation about our bodies, our development ☐
- ☐ being shamed for being male/female ☐
- ☐ exposure to pornography ☐
- ☐ sexualized comments ☐
- ☐ all forms of sexual abuse ☐
- ☐ engaging a person sexually without his or her permission ☐
- ☐ insisting on having your way sexually without respecting partner's discomfort ☐
- ☐ not respecting safe sex practices ☐
- ☐ sexually shaming another ☐
- ☐ being shamed for having same sex attraction ☐

**Emotional:**

☐ feelings denied ☐

☐ told what you can and cannot feel ☐

☐ being raged at ☐

☐ being criticized ☐

☐ being belittled ☐

☐ lack of expectations ☐

☐ being terrorized ☐

☐ interrupting ☐

☐ being made fun of ☐

☐ lying ☐

☐ being sarcastic ☐

☐ by word or deed, indicating that another person is worthless ☐

**Spiritual:**

☐ going against personal values or rights to please others ☐

☐ taught to believe in a punishing higher power ☐

☐ no spiritual guidance ☐

☐ no sense of prayer or gratitude ☐

**Relationship:**

☐ falling in love with anyone who reaches out ☐

☐ allowing someone to take as much as they can from you ☐

☐ letting others define your reality ☐

☐ believing others can anticipate your needs (mindreading) ☐

**Intellectual:**

☐ denied information ☐

☐ not allowed to make mistakes ☐

☐ not encouraged to question ☐

☐ being called stupid ☐

☐ encouraged to follow someone else's dream rather than your own ☐

## EXERCISE 95

You may want to keep a daily journal like the one below in which you identify times when you have tolerated intrusive behavior by others—or, if you need to work on the other side of that continuum, times when you have behaved in a manner that might have been intrusive to others. After completing each daily entry, note the feeling you experienced in relation to the situation. Do this exercise repeatedly. After completing this to the extent that you clearly identify such situations, identify the options available via words and/or behaviors that would be appropriate alternative responses. Repeat this for several situations.

Examples:

| Tolerated Inappropriate Behavior | Demonstrated Intrusive Behavior |
|---|---|
| I did not stick up for myself when my lover called me a name. | I assumed that my sister would babysit for me. I didn't ask ahead of time, although I knew I needed a sitter three days ago. |
| **Feeling or Attitude**: Hurt, humiliation, anger. | **Feeling or Attitude**: "She owes it to me, she's my sister." |
| **Alternative Behavior**: I could have said, "I am not a dumb so-and-so," then assert my position. OR I could have said, "It is difficult for me to understand your position when you call me names." | **Alternative Behavior**: Asking my sister if she was available at the time I became aware of my need. OR Never assume my sister is obligated to babysit for me, and always consider it a favor. When I ask her to babysit, I must understand that she has priorities of her own. |

*SAMPLE JOURNAL ENTRY:*                         **MONDAY**

| Tolerated Inappropriate Behavior | Demonstrated Intrusive Behavior |
|---|---|
| _____ _____ | _____ _____ |
| **Feeling or Attitude:** _____ _____ | **Feeling or Attitude:** _____ _____ |
| **Alternative Behavior:** _____ _____ | **Alternative Behavior:** _____ _____ |

## TOUCH

The following exercises can be extremely valuable in looking at the issue of touch in your life. If you experienced sexual molestation or physical abuse, it is suggested you only do these with the support and assistance of a trained helping professional.

If in doing these exercises you acknowledge for the first time you were sexually abused, it is important you share this information with someone you trust. It is also suggested you seek professional counseling. Similarly, if you are only now acknowledging having experienced physical abuse as a child, the power of this knowledge may also warrant seeking professional counseling. Both sexual molestation and physical abuse frequently repeat themselves generationally. Victims often continue to be victims of abuse, and sometimes even become sexual perpetrators and physical abusers themselves. Please seek professional attention immediately if you experience being drawn to or acting out in either capacity.

Touch is a vital aspect of human health and well-being. Touch is nurturing. It helps people feel connected, bonded, and loved.

People receive touch in a variety of ways. Positive touches include hugs, holding hands, pats on the back, a rub of the head, a hand on the shoulder, or sitting close to another.

Negative touches are slaps, pinches, kicks, punches, or being slammed against the wall.

Kisses can be negative or positive. Kisses hello or good night are generally positive, but some kisses may be associated with drunkenness, guilt, or manipulation.

Children may experience sexual energy with kisses, hugs, and being touched. This is confusing, scary, and can be guilt-inducing. Some children experience direct sexual contact with other family members—experiences in fondling, oral sex, anal sex, or intercourse. This is incest.

Sometimes there is simply no touching in a family.

## MEANING OF TOUCH

### EXERCISE 96

Please write about what touch represented to you as a child. Describe touch between you and your mother, between you and your father, between you and your siblings, and between you and any other family members or people outside of your family:

Mother: _____

_____

_____

_____

_____

Father: _____

_____

_____

_____

_____

Brothers (name individual brothers): _____

_____

_____

_____

_____

Sisters (name individual sisters):_____

_____

_____

_____

_____

Others: extended family members, neighbors and others (name):_____

_____

_____

_____

_____

# PICTURE OF TOUCH

## EXERCISE 97

Do a collage or draw a picture about what being touched represented to you as a child.

## EXAMPLE:

1) A picture of a woman hugging a child may represent that your mother hugged you a lot.
2) A picture of a school graduation may indicate you were only hugged at ceremonial events.
3) A picture of a large hand may represent that you were slapped with an open hand.
4) A picture of a teddy bear may represent that you were seldom touched and you used a stuffed animal for physical nurturing.

Refer back to Exercise 8 for instructions for creating a collage.

# TOUCHING PEOPLE

## EXERCISE 98

This exercise is for you to give thought to how you touch the people in your life—literally. Using the following words, note the style of touch you tend to use with people, male and female, recognizing that touch will vary with individual people:

| WORDS: | | | |
|---|---|---|---|
| | Kiss | Handshake | Slap |
| | Hug | No Touch | Hit |
| | Sexual | Pinch | Kick |
| | Pat (on arm, leg, shoulder, etc.) | | |

| PEOPLE | MALE | FEMALE |
|---|---|---|
| Acquaintances | _____ | _____ |
| Friends | _____ | _____ |
| Professional associates | _____ | _____ |

| PEOPLE | MALE | FEMALE |
|---|---|---|
| Parents | _____ | _____ |
| Brother/Sister (name) | | |
| _____ | _____ | _____ |
| _____ | _____ | _____ |
| _____ | _____ | _____ |
| _____ | _____ | _____ |
| Extended family members | _____ | _____ |
| | _____ | _____ |
| Spouse/Partner | _____ | _____ |
| Your children (name) | | |
| _____ | _____ | _____ |
| _____ | _____ | _____ |
| _____ | _____ | _____ |
| _____ | _____ | _____ |

**EXERCISE 99**

Are you comfortable with touching people? Would you like your touching to be different? If so, how and with whom? Explain:

_____

_____

_____

_____

_____

_____

_____

_____

_____

_____

_____

# APOLOGIES

It is common to hear people apologize yet continue their hurtful behavior, or hear someone apologize for the behavior of another, or not apologize at all when it is warranted.

The ability to offer and receive apologies is often influenced by what you experienced growing up.

**EXERCISE 100**

What did apologies mean in your family? Who apologized to whom? Were apologies sincere? Did anything positive come from apologies? Write about this:

_____

_____

_____

_____

_____

_____

_____

_____

_____

_____

_____

## PERPETUAL APOLOGIES

### EXERCISE 101

If you are a perpetual apologizer (a person who always apologizes), reflect on the instances as both a young person and as an adult, and note apologies you made that were inappropriate in that you were not at fault.

After you've listed situations where you apologized to try to "fix" a situation, go back to each time frame and note what you feared would have happened if you had not apologized. Examples:

| I apologized for: | My fear was if I didn't apologize . . . |
|---|---|
| The time my dad hit my brother. | No one else would help my brother feel better. |
| The time I told my husband that he was intimidating the kids by yelling at them all of the time. | My husband would quit talking altogether and I couldn't stand the quiet tension. |

| Ages | Apologies Made | Fear |
|------|----------------|------|
| Before 6 | _____ | _____ |
|  | _____ | _____ |
|  | _____ | _____ |
| 6–12 | _____ | _____ |
|  | _____ | _____ |
|  | _____ | _____ |
| 13–18 | _____ | _____ |
|  | _____ | _____ |
|  | _____ | _____ |
| 19–24 | _____ | _____ |
|  | _____ | _____ |
|  | _____ | _____ |
| 25–34 | _____ | _____ |
|  | _____ | _____ |
|  | _____ | _____ |
| 35–44 | _____ | _____ |
|  | _____ | _____ |
|  | _____ | _____ |
| 45–54 | _____ | _____ |
|  | _____ | _____ |
|  | _____ | _____ |

55–64        _____        _____

             _____        _____

             _____        _____

65 +         _____        _____

             _____        _____

             _____        _____

If you apologize for things for which you are not responsible, your focus needs to be on: 1) resolving guilt, which includes accepting your ability/inability to impact people and situations; 2) addressing your need for approval; 3) addressing your fears of rejection; and 4) addressing your fear of conflict.

## EXERCISE 102

To assist you in identifying situations in which you apologize inappropriately, finish the following statements:

I don't need to apologize for _____

_____

_____

I don't need to apologize for _____

_____

_____

I don't need to apologize for _____

_____

_____

I don't need to apologize for _____

_____

_____

# DIFFICULTY APOLOGIZING

## EXERCISE 103

This exercise is for the person who has difficulty apologizing. Using these time frames, reflect on things you did or said (not thoughts or feelings) for which you owe someone an apology:

An example would be:

| I didn't apologize for: | My belief or feeling that was an obstacle to apologizing |
|---|---|
| I haven't apologized to my daughter for not showing up at her school play. | The feeling that interfered was my anger with my ex-wife and my desire to make her angry. I prioritized my feelings toward my ex-wife over my love for my daughter. |
| I didn't apologize when I called my son a name. | The belief that interfered was that I would look weak if I did. |

| Ages | I didn't apologize for: | My belief or feeling that was an obstacle to apologizing |
|---|---|---|
| Before 6 | _____ | _____ |
|  | _____ | _____ |
|  | _____ | _____ |
| 6–12 | _____ | _____ |
|  | _____ | _____ |
|  | _____ | _____ |
| 13–18 | _____ | _____ |
|  | _____ | _____ |
| 19–24 | _____ | _____ |
|  | _____ | _____ |

25–34      _____          _____

           _____          _____

           _____          _____

35–44      _____          _____

           _____          _____

           _____          _____

45–54      _____          _____

           _____          _____

           _____          _____

55–64      _____          _____

           _____          _____

           _____          _____

65 +       _____          _____

           _____          _____

           _____          _____

Do you see any patterns that interfere with your willingness to apologize?

## EXERCISE 104

Using the following format, name the people to whom you owe apologies. Mark with a check (✓) those you can apologize to in person, on the phone, and/or in a letter. Mark with an X those to whom you still would not apologize. Note if the person is now deceased. Make your apology to the people whose names you have checked, and note the date.

Regarding those marked with an X, ask yourself what the belief or feeling is that keeps you from apologizing. Once that is identified, discuss this with someone you trust. After you've completed this process, go back to your list, and see if you can convert any of the Xs to "✓s."

| (✓)<br>Name of Person or Deceased<br>(X) | Nature of Apology | Date Accomplished |
|---|---|---|
| | | |

## APOLOGY LETTER

### EXERCISE 105

Should you want to apologize to a now-deceased person, do so in the form of a letter. Remember, there is no need to apologize for thoughts or feelings, only behaviors.

Dear _____,

I want to apologize for _____

_____

_____

I want to apologize for _____

_____

_____

I want to apologize for _____

_____

_____

I want to apologize for _____

_____

_____

Now that you have written the first letter, it's very important that you write a second letter to yourself from the deceased person. In this letter, this person will tell you that he/she forgives you for each infraction or instance for which you are apologizing.

Dear _____,

I forgive you for the time _____

_____

_____

I forgive you for the time _____

_____

_____

I forgive you for the time _____

_____

_____

I forgive you for the time _____

_____

_____

## GROUNDING: YOUR FIVE SENSES

Sit comfortably. Close your eyes or lower your gaze. Relax for a few moments. Take a few slow, deep breaths.

Open your eyes or lift your gaze when you are ready. Silently, one by one, identify five different things you see around you. Do this calmly and slowly.

Now silently identify four things you hear. Then identify three things you smell. Identify two things you taste. Lastly, name one thing you are touching.

Continue to be aware of your breathing as you go about your day.

# CHAPTER FIVE
# FROM MODERATION TO EXCESS

## COMPULSIVE BEHAVIOR

There are times when everyone needs escape mechanisms. However, when you come to rely on escape behaviors to relieve a chronic sense of unworthiness, those behaviors become compulsive in nature. Compulsive behaviors create distance between you and others, and separate you from your inner truth, interfering with your ability to be honest with yourself.

Patrick Carnes, in his work with sexual addiction, offers an acronym that can be helpful in identifying other compulsive behavior: S.A.F.E.

Secretive— Are you involved in a process or a behavior that is secretive? Is it something you do not want to talk about openly?

Abusive— Are you involved in a process or behavior that is abusive? Is it harmful or hurtful to yourself or another?

Feelings— Does this process or behavior separate you from your feelings? Does it numb or medicate your feelings? Or, is it the only time you experience feelings?

Emptiness— After you have engaged in it awhile, does this process or behavior leave you with a sense of emptiness?

Compulsive behaviors can involve work, eating, sex, relationships, making money, gambling, spending money, exercise, online activities/social media, video gaming, list making, or even television watching. While some of these areas of behavior are obviously more harmful than others, any of them can evolve into process forms of addiction when they become compulsive, and are used to alter feelings. If you are involved in a process or behavior that interferes with your ability to be honest with yourself, it deserves your attention.

## FOOD

People raised in unhappy homes and those who are unhappy will often eat for emotional reasons rather than for physical need. Food can become a source of nurturance providing a sense of comfort and solace. For others, eating morphs into a form of self-medicating, which often becomes unhealthy and self-destructive, encourages self-hatred, and leads to eating disorders. While most people who become self-destructive via food do this by binge eating and/or overeating, some people compensate for overeating by purging (deliberately inducing vomiting). When binging and purging becomes a pattern of behavior, people are diagnosed with bulimia nervosa. Others demonstrate self-destructiveness through a form of self-starvation that can lead to anorexia. For the anorexic, eating and food can carry a lot of symbolism. Not eating may reflect one's self-hatred and could be an act of punishment. It could be a desire to become invisible. Very often, it is an attempt to have control while feeling a lack of control in other areas of your life. Everyone needs to reflect on what food means to them. Should your relationship with food be a problem in your life, it is important that you seek help with a specialist in the field of disordered eating.

## EATING HABITS

### EXERCISE 106

As a child and teenager, I ate: (Circle one)

A great deal more          More than          An appropriate          Less than          Was often
than necessary             necessary          amount                  normal             hungry

If you ate more or less than normal, write about that. Why do you think this occurred? What did eating or not eating do for you?

_____

_____

_____

_____

Is your pattern of eating the same or different today? _____

If it is the same, what does eating or not eating do for you today? _____

_____

_____

_____

_____

If it is different, how has it changed? _____

_____

_____

_____

_____

## EXERCISE 107

What was your parents' attitude about weight?

Mom _____

Dad _____

What messages did your parents give you about what to eat?

Mom _____

Dad _____

What is your attitude about weight?

_____

_____

_____

Be aware that if you consistently eat out of loneliness, anger, fear, or to escape; if you eat to feel better and it's one of the few ways you know how to feel better, you may need additional help to find ways of expressing feelings, accepting yourself, and getting your needs met.

## MONEY

### EXERCISE 108

How you value money—the acquiring and spending of it—is often related to how money was acquired and spent in your family.

The following questions will help you to explore possible connections of the past to the present:

How did your father earn money? _____

Did you have any strong feelings about how he earned money or the amount that he earned?

_____

How did your father spend money? Did you have any strong feelings about his spending?

_____

_____

_____

Pertaining to both earning and spending:

I wished he would have _____

_____

_____

I wished he wouldn't have _____

_____

_____

## EXERCISE 109

How did your mother earn money? _____

Did you have any strong feelings about how she earned money or the amount that she earned?

_____

How did your mom spend money? Did you have any strong feelings about her spending?

_____

_____

_____

Pertaining to both earning and spending:

I wished she would have _____

_____

_____

I wished she wouldn't have _____

_____

_____

## EXERCISE 110

When did you first have your own money? How did you get it? What did you do with it?

_____

_____

_____

_____

_____

Were you embarrassed and wished your family had more or less money?

_____

_____

_____

If your family had more or less money, how would that have impacted you and your family?

_____

_____

_____

_____

_____

_____

# MONEY TODAY

## EXERCISE 111

Circle T for True or F for False to help you assess your present attitudes regarding money:

T  F   I hate to spend money.

T  F   I make sure I always pay my own way.

T  F   I seldom spend money on myself.

T  F   I seldom spend money on anyone else.

T  F   I can never keep any money; I spend whatever I have.

T  F   I am afraid of not having enough money.

T  F   I have no strong feelings about money—positive or negative.

Describe your financial situation today:

_____

_____

_____

_____

_____

_____

Do you have any financial fears? Explain:

_____

_____

_____

_____

_____

_____

_____

_____

_____

_____

_____

### EXERCISE 112

How similar or dissimilar are your financial issues to those of your parents? Explain your answer.

_____

_____

_____

_____

_____

_____

_____

_____

_____

# WORK

### EXERCISE 113

Did your parents work outside of the home? If so, what type of work did they do? Did they appear to enjoy their work? What gave you that impression? What were their work habits?

Mother _____

_____

_____

_____

Father _____

_____

_____

_____

If either parent was a stay-at-home parent, what were her (his) work habits? Did she or he appear to enjoy being at home? What gave you that impression?

_____

_____

_____

What beliefs did you internalize about work? For example:
- Work is what you do to pay bills.
- You work to get by.
- Work gives your life meaning.
- Let others do the work.
- Work can be enjoyable.

Other: _____

_____

_____

Describe your work pattern as an adult: _____

_____

_____

How do your beliefs reinforce that pattern? _____

_____

_____

_____

Does the way in which you work interfere with other aspects of your life, e.g. health, relationships with children, with partner, etc.?

_____

_____

_____

_____

_____

## SUBSTANCE USE

Becoming dependent on alcohol and other drugs is an insidious process. For many people alcohol and other drugs start out as a solution, the answer for inner emptiness and driving emotional pain. While many people are able to use alcohol and other drugs without becoming addicted, approximately 12 percent of people who use alcohol and other drugs will become addicted. Total abstinence from alcohol and drugs is the only defense against the potential for addiction.

Most people use alcohol or other drugs believing that they have the self-control and willpower to avoid addiction. However, the best intentions, self-control, and intelligence won't keep you from becoming addicted. While it can happen to anyone, addiction is most prevalent in families when it is generational, with a genetic predisposition, and when there is a history of trauma.

The following three questions are important to ask yourself:
- Do you use alcohol or other drugs to have fun?
- Do you use alcohol or other drugs to relax?
- Do you use alcohol or other drugs to escape?

These are common reasons for using alcohol and other drugs, but if you answered "yes" to these three questions it does not necessarily mean you have a problem. Answering the following questions will provide additional clues about whether drinking or other drug usage may become a problem for you.

1. Do you find ways to have fun that don't include using alcohol or other drugs? (Some people may say, "Sure, I bowl." But is it common that the bowling is rewarded afterwards by getting drunk?)
2. Do you find ways to relax that don't include using alcohol or other drugs? (Some people say that they watch videos to relax, and forget to mention that they light up a joint several times in the process.)
3. Do you have other avenues of escape that don't include using alcohol or other drugs? (Again, this requires total honesty.)

If you answer no to any of the above questions, I suggest you take this as a serious signal of the need for you to begin to work on finding alternative forms of fun, relaxation, or escape. If you answered no to two or three of the questions, it is suggested you seek help to explore your use of alcohol and other drugs.

## PHYSICAL SELF-CARE

### EXERCISE 114

Physical self-care means attending to your physical needs. To what extent do you eat healthy foods, drink enough water, exercise, and maintain a healthy weight?

What were your models for physical self-care? _____

_____

_____

_____

Describe your pattern of physical self-care: _____

_____

_____

_____

Would you like to change? _____

_____

_____

_____

What beliefs or behaviors sabotage this potential change? _____

_____

_____

_____

What do you need to support your physical self-care practice? _____

_____

_____

_____

## GROUNDING: PALMS UP, PALMS DOWN

Sit comfortably, with your back straight but not stiff. (You may find this easier if you sit on the front edge of a chair, rather than against the back.)

Close your eyes or lower your gaze.

Bring your attention to your breathing.

Take a slow, deep breath. As you do, count to four slowly—one, two, three, four—at the rate of about two numbers per second.

Then exhale, counting slowly to four once again.

Do this again. And keep repeating until your breathing is slow and relaxed.

As you continue to breathe slowly and evenly, hold your hands out in front of you with your palms facing up. Leave your elbows at your sides or stretch out your arms fully—whatever feels more comfortable.

Imagine your hands holding all the difficult thoughts, feelings, and events that you experienced today. Feel their weight.

Now turn your palms down. Imagine all the troubling energy you have been carrying dropping to the ground.

Turn your empty palms back up. They are now ready to receive positive energy, supportive thoughts, good feelings, and help from others. Hold your palms in this position for ten to twenty seconds.

Slowly open your eyes.

# CHAPTER SIX
# RITUALS & SPIRITUAL INFLUENCES

## RITUALS

Family rituals offer an opportunity for knitting relationships more closely together; for conveying positive family identity; creating a sense of belonging to a unit with a past, a present, and a future, and connecting to a larger community or culture.

Unfortunately, for many people, family rituals are times of great upheaval. So often there are arguments, silent tension, drunkenness, missing relatives, grotesquely inappropriate gifts, forced smiles, and cold, superficial, or hollow interchanges. Creating or redesigning new rituals can do much to make up for the past, create a positive present, and move toward a more hopeful future.

## HOLIDAYS

Holidays are supposed to be happy and festive, but in reality they are often a time of anxiety and depression. A reason for this is that holidays are occasions when families get together. Family gatherings on holidays imply that everyone must have a good time. Yet this is very difficult to accomplish if you grew up in an environment of dishonesty, unexpressed feelings, grief, and abuse.

In families where wearing masks is a general rule, there is a greater need for masks on days that are designated for being together and celebrating, giving and receiving, having fun, and relaxing.

For addicted families, three-day weekends such as July Fourth, Labor Day, or Memorial Day frequently mean three days of drinking and drugging vs. two days.

Valentine's Day may represent another time Dad gets to forget Mom.

Easter may represent the one time a year when the family goes to church.

Passover means waiting to see if Mom stays sober or gets drunk before the holiday dinner.

Christmas may mean needing to give Dad a present after he has slapped you around all year.

Holidays can certainly be happy times, but as a rule of thumb, they are much more compromised in impaired families.

## EXERCISE 115

Using the following list, write the words that best describe what family holidays mean to you (add words of your own, if you wish):

| | | | | |
|---|---|---|---|---|
| depression | giving | food | happiness | presents |
| receiving | drinking | excitement | fun | violence |
| intoxication | loneliness | vacation | party | picnic |
| fear | guilt | sadness | boredom | games |

|  | As a Child | As an Adult |
|---|---|---|
| 1. New Year's | _____ | _____ |
|  | _____ | _____ |
|  | _____ | _____ |
| 2. Easter | _____ | _____ |
|  | _____ | _____ |
|  | _____ | _____ |
| 3. Memorial Day | _____ | _____ |
|  | _____ | _____ |
|  | _____ | _____ |
| 4. July 4th | _____ | _____ |
|  | _____ | _____ |
|  | _____ | _____ |

|              | As a Child | As an Adult |
| ------------ | ---------- | ----------- |

5. Labor Day

6. Thanksgiving

7. Christmas

8. Holiday(s) specific to your culture

a.

b.

c.

## CHRISTMAS (PAST)

While this is written to focus on Christmas, pick whatever holiday is significant for you and use the same format to explore your experience with it.

### EXERCISE 116

Christmas is often a difficult time for people. The following exercises will help you explore old issues around this holiday:

1. Christmas was a time of _____

_____

_____

2. At Christmas time, my father _____

_____

_____

3. At Christmas time, my mother_____

_____

_____

4. At Christmas time, I _____

_____

_____

5. At Christmas time, my brother_____

_____

_____

6. At Christmas time, my brother _____

_____

_____

7. At Christmas time, my sister _____

_____

_____

8. At Christmas time, my sister _____

_____

_____

9. The best part of the holiday was _____

_____

_____

10. The worst part of the holiday was _____

_____

_____

# CHRISTMAS (PRESENT)

Again, if Christmas is not what you celebrate, pick the holiday that is significant to you and your faith.

## EXERCISE 117

What is Christmas like for you now?

1. Christmas is a time of _____

_____

_____

_____

_____

_____

_____

_____

_____

2. The best part of the holiday is_____

_____

_____

3. The worst part of the holiday is _____

_____

_____

If you are happy with your Christmas experience today, you may go on to the next exercise. Otherwise, complete the following:

I'd like Christmas to be a time when_____

_____

_____

In order for that to happen, I would have to _____

_____

_____

Am I willing to do the above?        Yes        No        Partially

If "no," what is my fear? _____

_____

_____

What do I need to work on in order to make it a "yes"? _____

_____

_____

_____

_____

_____

_____

_____

# BIRTHDAYS

## EXERCISE 118

Check "yes" or "no" in response to each of the following statements:        YES        NO

Birthdays are to be celebrated.        _____   _____

Birthdays are just another day.        _____   _____

Birthdays are for kids.        _____   _____

Birthdays are great, as long as they're not mine.        _____   _____

I hate my birthday.        _____   _____

|                                    | YES          | NO           |
|------------------------------------|--------------|--------------|
| I like my birthday.                | _____     | _____     |
| I feel special on my birthday.     | _____     | _____     |
| I try to forget my birthday.       | _____     | _____     |

Other thoughts: _____

_____

## EXERCISE 119

Write about any two birthdays before your twentieth birthday that were positive, and for that reason stand out for you:

_____

_____

_____

_____

_____

_____

Now, write about any two birthdays before your twentieth birthday that you remember with sadness, disappointment, or anger:

_____

_____

_____

_____

_____

_____

_____

_____

_____

As an adult, describe your attitude regarding birthdays for the past ten years:

_____

_____

_____

_____

_____

_____

Do any one or two of your birthdays during the last ten years stand out as particularly fun, happy, or special?

Which ones? _____ , _____

Explain what made them special:

_____

_____

_____

Do any one or two of your birthdays during the last ten years stand out as particularly unhappy? If so, which ones?

_____ , _____

Explain what made them unhappy:

_____

_____

_____

_____

## EXERCISE 120

Regarding your next birthday, list three ways that you can make that day a special one for you:

1. _____

_____

2. _____

_____

3. _____

_____

# GIFT GIVING AND RECEIVING

## EXERCISE 121

What were your models for gift giving and receiving? What messages were you given about both giving and receiving? Thoughts to consider: Who gave to whom? Was it obligatory, thoughtful, spontaneous, and/or creative?

_____

_____

_____

_____

_____

_____

_____

_____

_____

How is the giving and receiving of gifts different for you today, or how would you like it to be different for you?

_____

_____

_____

_____

_____

_____

_____

_____

## BEDTIME

### EXERCISE 122

Bedtime carries with it a variety of memories. Most children have a consistent bedtime that gets later as they grow older. Many children know their bedtime and get themselves to bed, often with only slight prodding by their parents. Children often say "goodnight" to their parents, and when they are young, perhaps that "goodnight" is accompanied by a kiss. But in impaired families, bedtimes are stressful. Children often have inappropriate bedtimes such as 8:00 p.m. for a fifteen-year-old or 11:00 p.m. for a seven-year-old. Children may not have any consistent structure for bedtime, and are left to decide when they go to bed with lights out. Consequently, they don't get the amount of sleep they need. You may have gone to bed sad, afraid, angry, and lonely. You may have found yourself taking your pet, food, or imaginary friends to bed with you for comfort. You may have been one of those kids who would stay up at night waiting for a parent to come home or lying awake while listening to family members fighting. Compulsive praying may be a bedtime ritual when seeking relief from your grief or anxiety.

What was bedtime like for you between the ages of:

Before 6 _____

_____

_____

_____

_____

6–10 _____

_____

_____

_____

11–14 _____

_____

_____

_____

15–18 _____

_____

_____

_____

What is bedtime like for you now? Do you have an approximate time each night that you retire to bed? Do you fall asleep elsewhere in the house first before going to bed? Do you keep lights on? Do you say prayers? Do your animals sleep with you?

_____

_____

_____

_____

_____

_____

_____

## DINNER

Dinnertime means different things to different people. Examples:
- A time when the family could get together to share the day's experiences with each other.
- A time when Mom often worried about where Dad was.
- A time of silent tension.
- A time of arguing.

## EXERCISE 123

Complete the sentences:

Growing up, dinner was a time _____

_____

Growing up, dinner was a time _____

_____

Growing up, dinner was a time _____

_____

Please circle the appropriate response:

| | | |
|---|---|---|
| Was dinner looked forward to? | YES | NO |
| Was it a time to socialize? | YES | NO |
| Was it usually a positive time? | YES | NO |
| Was there often arguing? | YES | NO |
| Did people tend to "eat and run"? | YES | NO |
| Did people eat at different times? | YES | NO |
| Did people eat together? | YES | NO |
| Was the time of dinner fairly regular? | YES | NO |
| Was the responsibility for dinner, including cleanup, shared among the entire family? | YES | NO |

# DINNERTIME PICTURE

## EXERCISE 124

Draw a picture or do a collage that typifies what dinnertime was like at your house when you were a child. Give thought to the location, who sat next to whom, what you typically had to eat, the topic of dinner conversation, who did the talking, and the overall dinnertime mood.

EXAMPLES:

1) A picture of a table setting represents dinner being a time when all family members come together.

2) A picture of a kitchen table loaded with food represents the meals that you didn't have.

3) A picture of a traffic signal represents that family members took turns speaking and listening to each other when eating.

Refer back to Exercise 8 to refresh yourself on instructions for creating a collage.

## EXERCISE 125

Complete the following:

As an adult, dinner is a time of _____

_____

As an adult, dinner is a time of _____

_____

As an adult, dinner is a time of _____

_____

Please circle the appropriate response:

As an adult, do I look forward to dinner?                    YES          NO

Is it a time to socialize?                                   YES          NO

| | | |
|---|---|---|
| Is it usually a positive time? | YES | NO |
| Is there often arguing? | YES | NO |
| Do people "eat and run" (present family)? | YES | NO |
| Do people eat at different times (present family)? | YES | NO |
| Do people eat together (present family)? | YES | NO |
| Is dinnertime fairly consistent? | YES | NO |
| Is cleanup and the responsibility for dinner shared among the entire family? | YES | NO |

## EXERCISE 126

Describe a wonderful dinner:

_____

_____

_____

_____

_____

_____

_____

_____

What will it take for you to have dinner like that?

_____

_____

_____

_____

_____

_____

_____

_____

_____

Give yourself a time frame to accomplish the above, and then make that wonderful dinner a reality.

# RELIGION

To heal from pain and conflict in your life you need to have faith in something outside of yourself. Otherwise, you don't recover. Your faith may be in a "Higher Power" or "God." Possibly you aren't sure. While you may be agnostic or have little faith in anything outside yourself, be open to the possibility that faith can be of value for you and try to develop faith in a process. Trust that in time healing, self-love, and love of others can become a part of your life.

### EXERCISE 127

Whether or not you were raised with the influence of a particular religion or faith, most people share the concept of God in some form.

What church, mosque or synagogue did you attend as a child? _____

_____

If you were involved in religion as a child, describe your involvement by circling Yes or No. Was it:

| | | |
|---|---|---|
| Fun? | YES | NO |
| Scary? | YES | NO |
| Boring? | YES | NO |
| Meaningful? | YES | NO |

Was your concept of God (circle one):        LOVING        PUNISHING        INDIFFERENT

Other_____

Explain _____

_____

_____

_____

_____

_____

_____

Did you attend a church, mosque, or synagogue only because your parents dictated your involvement? YES   NO

## EARLY RELIGIOUS INFLUENCE

### EXERCISE 128

As a child or teenager, were there any particular religious rituals or ceremonies that were of special significance for you? What were they and how were they special?

_____

_____

_____

_____

_____

_____

_____

_____

_____

_____

_____

_____

_____

_____

## EXERCISE 129

Looking back at your early religious influence, what parts are positive that are still with you today?

_____

_____

_____

_____

_____

_____

_____

Are there any negative influences still with you?

_____

_____

_____

_____

_____

_____

_____

## RELIGION TODAY

### EXERCISE 130

Are you currently involved in the religion in which you were raised?      YES      NO

If not, what made you discontinue your involvement?

_____

_____

_____

_____

_____

Describe your feelings about religion today:

_____

_____

_____

_____

_____

Would you like to go back to your original faith?          YES     NO

Explain:_____

_____

_____

_____

_____

If you are active in a twelve-step program, describe your relationship with a "Higher Power":

_____

_____

_____

_____

_____

_____

_____

_____

_____

_____

_____

_____

_____

_____

_____

_____

## SPIRITUAL JOURNEY

### EXERCISE 131

Check any of the phrases that describe your spiritual pathway.

| | |
|---|---|
| Music / singing | _____ |
| Quiet, solitude | _____ |
| Appreciating nature | _____ |
| Loving others unselfishly | _____ |
| Listening to others | _____ |
| Sharing your feelings | _____ |
| Keeping a journal | _____ |
| Forgiving others | _____ |
| Attending a church, synagogue, or other place of worship | _____ |
| Praising others | _____ |
| Smiling, laughing | _____ |
| Reading, learning | _____ |

Helping others                    _____

Sharing experiences               _____

Asking for forgiveness            _____

Embracing loved ones              _____

Twelve Steps                      _____

Meditation                        _____

Other Spiritual practice          _____

## GRATITUDE LIST

Research about gratitude has occurred over centuries, and over the last decade it has shown us that adults who feel grateful have more energy, more optimism, more social connections, and more happiness than those who do not. They're also less likely to be stressed, depressed, anxious, greedy or active addicts.

Because gratitude encourages us not only to appreciate gifts but also to repay them (or pay them forward), the sociologist Georg Simmel called it "the moral memory of mankind."

### EXERCISE 132

Complete the sentences:

Today I am grateful for:

_____

_____

_____

Today I am grateful for:

_____

_____

_____

Today I am grateful for

_____

_____

_____


On a daily basis find a moment to acknowledge your gratitude.


## GROUNDING: CONNECTING TO A HIGHER POWER

The purpose of this meditation is to focus on developing a spiritual connection with yourself and your Higher Power. To walk the road of recovery requires patience and dedication to your spiritual program. It will be important as you continue on your recovery journey to develop your spiritual connection on a daily basis. Many in recovery do this through prayer and meditation.

The beginning of Step Eleven in twelve-step programs states: *Sought through prayer and meditation to improve our conscious contact with God **as we understood Him** . . .*

There are many wonderful daily meditation books that you may find useful. Some participants in recovery work on developing their own meditations and prayers. These usually involve visualizing their own Higher Power and also visualizing soothing and spiritual places—the beach, the mountains, the forest, etc.

*Gently sit back and close your eyes. Begin to breathe slowly and deeply. Focus on your breathing.*

*Take a deep breath in . . . and out. Take a deep breath in . . . and out. As you breathe in, visualize your Higher Power filling you with healing and protective light. As you breathe out, visualize stress, tension, worry, and fear leaving your body. Continue to breathe in and out.*

*Slowly become aware of your head and neck. Feel your tension melting away and feel your head and neck begin to relax. Feel this relaxation slowly moving down through your shoulders as you continue to breathe in healing light and energy. Feel the relaxation move down into your arms and chest. Know that you are safe and you are loved.*

*Breathe in . . . and out. Breathe in . . . and out.*

*Feel the relaxation moving down into your waist and legs. Feel the tension and stress leaving your body. Feel the relaxation moving down into your feet. Feel your connection to the earth and the connection to your Higher Power.*

*As you continue to breathe deeply, imagine a place where you feel completely safe and serene. This may be the mountains, the beach, or the forest. Wherever this place is, it is yours. Imagine yourself there right now. Take a look around and focus on what you see.*

*What do you smell?*

*What do you hear?*

*Let all of your senses experience the serenity and safety of this special place.*

*Know that this is your place that you can come to at any time.*

*Slowly begin to visualize how your Higher Power might look and feel. Let the image begin to fill your mind, body, and spirit.*

*Imagine your body and spirit being filled with serenity, contentment, and peace.*

*Feel your spirit connecting with your Higher Power. Feel the infinite wisdom and love your Higher Power has for you. Feel the safety and protection it offers you.*

*Know that your Higher Power guides your path in recovery and is with you at all times.*

*Know that you can connect with your Higher Power and your safe place any time you choose to through prayer and meditation.*

*Know that you are not alone in your recovery. You are surrounded by love and support if you choose to let it in.*

*As you continue to breathe, gently become aware of your body. Become aware of your head . . . your neck . . . your shoulders and arms. Become aware of your back . . . your chest . . . your waist . . . your legs . . . your feet. Become aware of your connection to the earth. When you are ready, open your eyes.*

Remember that the purpose of this imagery is to help you visualize and connect with your Higher Power. Each day through prayer and meditation you are able to feel this sense of connection and guidance from a Power greater than yourself. Spiritual fitness, like physical fitness, requires dedication.

# CHAPTER SEVEN
# EMBRACING THE POSSIBILITIES

You are at a wonderful place to begin to look at the risks that you may want to take that support you in recovery, to validate your accomplishments and look at your future with hope and intention, and lastly to recognize what you are letting go of and what you are taking with you in this journey.

## TAKING RISKS

### EXERCISE 133

List five risks you have taken in the past that you feel good about. They could be risks at work, in your family, or other relationships. These risks might be intellectual, physical, spiritual, or emotional.

1. Name the risk _____

What did you fear? _____

What did you do to push through the fear? What did you think, say, or do to get yourself to take the risk?

_____

_____

_____

_____

2. Name the risk _____

What did you fear? _____

What did you do to push through the fear? What did you think, say, or do to get yourself to take the risk?

_____

_____

_____

_____

3. Name the risk _____

What did you fear? _____

What did you do to push through the fear? What did you think, say, or do to get yourself to take the risk?

_____

_____

_____

_____

4. Name the risk _____

What did you fear? _____

What did you do to push through the fear? What did you think, say, or do to get yourself to take the risk?

_____

_____

_____

_____

5. Name the risk _____

What did you fear?_____

What did you do to push through the fear? What did you think, say, or do to get yourself to take the risk?

_____

_____

_____

_____

Now, name five risks you want to take. These risks may allow you to move closer to overall wellness, clear up areas of conflict or confusion, or pursue an alternative to a specific problem. Identify those risks and then answer the same questions.

1. Name the risk _____

What do you fear? _____

What do you need to do to push through the fear? What do you need to think, say, or do to get yourself to take the risk?

_____

_____

_____

_____

2. Name the risk _____

What do you fear? _____

What do you need to do to push through the fear? What do you need to think, say, or do to get yourself to take the risk?

_____

_____

_____

_____

3. Name the risk _____

What do you fear? _____

What do you need to do to push through the fear? What do you need to think, say, or do to get yourself to take the risk?

_____

_____

_____

_____

4. Name the risk _____

What do you fear? _____

What do you need to do to push through the fear? What do you need to think, say, or do to get yourself to take the risk?

_____

_____

_____

_____

5. Name the risk _____

What do you fear? _____

What did you need to do to push through the fear? What do you need to think, say, or do to get yourself to take the risk?

_____

_____

_____

_____

# TIMELINE OF ACCOMPLISHMENT

## EXERCISE 134

Create your own timeline. On a blank piece of paper draw a horizontal line. Note on the left end the date you were born. Then note on the right end the approximate time frame that you suspect this life will come to a close. Then note where you presently are in age. The following is an example of someone born in 1987, thirty years-of-age, who expects to live until their late eighties:

October                                                                                                    Late
1987 --------------------------------30 --------------------------------------------------------------------80s

Then, from your birth to today note your accomplishments. Recognize accomplishments are both internal and external. Examples include:
- Learning to walk
- Learning to ride a bicycle
- Learning to read
- High school graduation
- Marriage
- Divorce
- Raising a healthy and fun child
- Being technologically savvy
- No longer being a victim in life
- Recovery from depression/anxiety/addiction

This can be fun and very meaningful so take time to do this. You can even use pictures to portray accomplishments, or draw symbols.

When done, give thought to the latter part of your life and note:

What would you like to witness before you die?

What would you like to learn?

What would you like to see?

What would you like to be a part of?

Some examples might be:

- To travel to all seven continents of the world
- To see my children have the finances to go to college
- To run a marathon
- To spend time walking in the woods
- To develop a better relationship with my father
- To participate in animal rights advocacy

## THE MAGIC SHOP

### EXERCISE 135

Different from the other exercises in this workbook, this one requires that you read the exercise, digest and understand it, and then allow your mind to walk through this journey. Put yourself in a relaxed and quiet setting where you will not be interrupted. Check your breathing—breathe deeply in and out, in and out. Relax your muscles. Uncross your legs and arms to open yourself and stimulate blood circulation and energy. Allow your eyes to close.

*Let your mind wander to a place that represents safety to you. This is a place of safety that is nurturing for you. Now, in thought, take yourself to that place. This is a favorite spot of yours. It could be your backyard, the woods, the local park, the beach, out on a boat in a lake or river, or strolling through the streets of a favorite village. It is a fine day, the weather is as you like it, and you are in one of your favorite places.*

*In your special place you notice a small shop tucked away, in between other buildings, or amid the trees, in the corner of your closet, in the glove compartment of your car—wherever, this imaginary place becomes real. Its windows are dusty, and you do not remember seeing it before. You approach it and peer inside. There you see all kinds of things you have never imagined seeing in one place. It is a wonderful junk shop, flea market, antique shop, and specialty shop all rolled into one. With excited anticipation you open the door and notice that in the back of this store, behind a counter, waits a very Wise Old Person who feels most familiar to you.*

*As you approach, the Wise Old Person tells you this is a place where you can realize your dreams if you wish. What you get to do in this shop is to select an item from its shelves that symbolizes some positive change you wish to accomplish in your life and take it with you. In its place you must leave an old habit, feeling, job, person, or grief issue you no longer wish to have in your life. Because this is a magic shop, anything can be taken in exchange for anything you wish to leave.*

*Take your time looking around for just the right object or symbol you wish to take with you—courage, strength to set limits, greater playfulness, creativity, self-esteem, etc.—and think carefully about what it is you wish to leave behind that is dysfunctional or painful to you, such as anger, fear, a hurtful relationship, critical self-talk, and so forth. Take as much time as you need, wandering around the shop looking at all of the wonderful items and mulling over what it is you wish to take with you and what to leave behind in exchange.*

*When you are ready, put your unwanted item on the shelf and take in its place the item you want most to symbolize this change you are about to make in your life. Take a few moments to tell the Wise Old Person what it is you are leaving behind and what it is you are taking and what they each mean to you. When you are ready, thank this Wise Old Person. Carrying your new item, you leave the shop to find yourself back in your favorite place, allowing yourself to slowly and easily come back to the reality of the present.*

You may find it helpful to share this experience with someone and/or write about what you took, what you left behind, and the process of making those decisions.

## IN CLOSING

It is likely that weeks and perhaps months have passed since you first picked up *Repeat After Me* and began your process of reflection. You may find it helpful to do some of the exercises a second or third time over the next year or two. Change is an ongoing process and takes time. Be patient with yourself. Be willing to recognize your strengths. Find support systems to validate your feelings and perceptions. Begin to risk more of yourself. Try new behaviors that allow your needs to be met. Take responsibility for how you live your life today.

Today, you deserve:

To play

To laugh

To relax

To be flexible

To develop the ability to lead yet feel comfortable when it is time to follow

To question

To talk honestly

To make decisions

To attend to your own needs

To understand where your power lies

To protect yourself

To know and accept your feelings and to be able to express those feelings

To no longer live your life in fear

And to believe in your specialness.

9 781942 094777